Contents

Foreword by Gary Lineker 6

1   Born Black and White 8

2   The London Alternative 18

3   Biking to the Baggies 30

4   The Young International 40

5   Back at the Cottage 52

6   The Champagne Years 62

7   The Best Job in the World 100

8   An Englishman Abroad 150

9   Bobby Five O 162

10 The Buffer Zone 172

11 The Homecoming 190

12 The Final Chapter 224

Career Record 234

Index and Acknowledgements 236

Foreword by Gary Lineker

I always felt Sir Bobby Robson had a great story to tell. He enjoyed a remarkably successful career and was just as popular at the end of his life as he was in the early days, right across the country. But it was not just about his successes on the football pitch, but as a person. He was always so enthusiastic and so passionate. He was a real people's person, as he showed towards the end of his life, where even though he was very ill, he put so much into his cancer charity. His is a good story, which was one of the reasons why I wanted to help tell it. So often these days people want to nit-pick, find people's weaknesses and dig out their faults, whereas this is just looking back at someone's very successful life.

I met Bobby for the first time when he called me up for England when I was at Leicester City. I was messing about at home when I had a call from our manager, Gordon Milne, who said, "Pack yourself a toothbrush, come in and pick up your boots, you've got to get yourself up to Wrexham because Bobby Robson has been on the phone." I was instantly terrified at the thought of meeting up with one of my heroes, but what you got with Bobby was a real warmth. He made you feel at home and your first impressions of him were your lasting ones; he was a man who lived and loved and breathed football, a totally passionate man. He lived for the game, and he gave so much to the game.

As with most successful managers there was always a slightly eccentric side to Bobby. He was slightly quirky. He used to find you in training and he would spot things when they weren't quite right. He would have a little pop at you, and then he would bring you back up with the arm around the shoulder. He usually got the best out of individuals, because he was fiercely loyal and he would give the players a great deal of respect and ultimately he was the sort of guy you wanted to perform for. His man management was always good and his judgement of a player was as good as anybody's. You can see that with a lot of his buys and the people he brought in over the years.

SIR BOBBY ROBSON

Living the Game

BOB HARRIS

WEIDENFELD & NICOLSON

England Heroes.
(Left to right) Gary Lineker, Sir Bobby Robson and Paul Gascoigne.

For someone so amiable he was incredibly strong-willed. He wasn't the sort of bloke who was easily influenced. He knew who the best players were and he always had great convictions behind his decisions. I don't think he was ever influenced by the madness of the media, nor by so-called "player power". There was a great myth that it was player power that picked the team to play Holland in the 1990 World Cup. But it wasn't true.

Towards the end of his life, even though he had serious health problems, that didn't in the slightest way dim his passion or his enthusiasm for football. He was still involved right up to the end. Recently I was privileged to present him with a lifetime achievement award and I found that a very emotive evening. There wasn't a dry eye in the house. It was quite something, a fitting tribute, and something that Bobby really deserved.

I consider myself very fortunate to have peaked in an era when Bobby was manager of England, and I will always be eternally grateful and privileged to have known him.

1   Born Black and White

The North East of England has always been a hotbed of football and the old story that you only had to whistle down the pit face to find a centre forward was not far off the mark.

Robert William Robson was born in the heart of the mining community in the little village of Sacriston, County Durham, on 18 February 1933. He moved soon afterwards to Langley Park and a two-up, two-down terrace house where he lived with his father, Philip, his mother, Lillian, and his four brothers: Tom, Philip, Ronald and Keith.

Bobby's father Philip was, of course, a miner and, naturally, a Newcastle United fan. The Robsons were fortunate, for, although Philip was a slightly built man, he must have been remarkably fit, because in fifty-one years at the coalface he missed just one shift, an extraordinary record and of immense benefit to his family for, in those days, if you did not work there was no such thing as sick pay.

"My father, Philip, was black and white, he bled black and white."

Lillian, as was customary, stayed at home to look after the five boys, and washed and ironed, cleaned and cooked.

It was tight in terms of money but, because every family in Langley Park lived on the same sort of budget, Bobby and his brothers didn't really notice. Everyone lived simply but well, passing down clothes from child to child. There were no televisions, and entertainment for the Robson boys and their friends was to play cricket with a lump of wood and an old, bald tennis ball or, more often, to play football with whatever was lying around, preferably an old leather football with its skin-ripping lace or, failing that, a piece of coal. That was one commodity they were not short of in Langley Park.

For the adults to entertain themselves there were a couple of football pitches, two cinemas - one of which later became a dance hall - pubs, an ice cream parlour and the Working Men's Club. Pints of strong ale were part of the culture after hours of working underground breathing in the coal dust – but not for the

A young Bobby photographed with his father, Philip, and mother, Lillian.

9

The Robson brothers
(from left to right):
Bobby (seated), Ron,
Phil and Keith.

Robsons. Philip was a teetotaller and a non-smoker. He and Lillian were strong Methodists and lived their life accordingly. Their frugality, however, brought good rewards for the boys, as they were among the few who could afford regular summer holidays, catching the coach to the local resort of Whitley Bay and, later, even to Blackpool as Philip earned promotion and with it a salary increase.

Entertainment in the Robson house was a radiogram (a combined radio and record player), which was loved by all the family, who regularly contributed to buy the old 78 rpm records by legends such as Frank Sinatra, Judy Garland, Bing Crosby and Nat King Cole. Bobby has always had a fine singing voice, and the influence of these early years was often heard throughout his career.

The other great diversion was Newcastle United. Sir Bobby has made no secret throughout his life that he " bled black and white". He and his father shared the passion of their fellow Geordies, and every other Saturday they would make their way to St James' Park, queue with the other fans hours before the gates opened, and then huddle on the terraces to watch heroes such as Len Shackleton, Albert Stubbins and Jackie Milburn.

These great football stars, along with his father, were the inspiration for the young Bobby to take up the game himself. He soon progressed from playing in the streets around his home to playing for his school side, Waterhouses Modern Intermediate, in games organized by his PE master, David Gilliland. These were specially arranged, as, quite incredibly considering the local community's avid following of the game, the school did not have a competitive football side. But the village did, and this talented young footballer was soon playing for Langley Park Juniors with lads much older than himself, turning out for the juniors in the

10

morning before racing off with his dad to watch his beloved Newcastle United in the afternoon. This hectic schedule was only interrupted when Bobby, aged fifteen, was picked to play for the Langley Park Under-18 side, who competed on Saturday afternoon, thus preventing Bobby's 34-mile round trip to Newcastle.

Bobby had little time to enjoy his childhood and, like so many other children at his secondary school, he was ejected into the daunting world of work at the age of fourteen-and-a-half. There was no question of where to work; it was off to the coalface with his father, now an overman, and his elder brother, Tom, an engineer. Bobby started not as a miner but as an apprentice electrician, which sounds like an easy vocation compared with the gruelling work of the pick-wielding miners, but it wasn't that easy. For a year and a half Bobby donned helmet, lamp and boots and went down the mine with the rest of the crew to repair the lights and other electrical fittings that had been damaged in the cramped and dusty passages.

Those eighteen months stood Bobby in good stead, and to this day he is appreciative of the work others have to do and of the value of money. He is not a mean man, far from it, but you would not find him wasting his money unnecessarily. As with his father, Philip, alcohol and tobacco held no interest at all, and even later he would smoke only the occasional cigar until he found out, along with the rest of his generation, the truth about the detrimental effects of tobacco. It was much the same with alcohol, and he only drinks the occasional glass of sparkling white wine.

Working down the pit also meant that when Bobby did break into the professional game he was able to appreciate the fact that he was doing something he loved for a living, which isn't often the case these days when a young player goes straight from school to club. Years later, before an away game against Derby County, he took the board of Ipswich Town to the local pit in Swadlincote, where his brother Tom was working. They were dressed up in overalls and hard hats, were given lamps, and were shown another side of life.

Despite working hard down the mine, Robson's football talent was fast emerging and attracting the attention of teams from across the country. Clubs as far apart as Southampton and Middlesbrough invited him for trials and both offered him pre-professional registration in 1948.

In the end he decided to sign for his local side, Middlesbrough, but became so disillusioned with their lack of interest in his development that, when they offered him a professional contract two years later, at the age of seventeen, he turned them down. By then he was well into his apprenticeship as an electrical engineer, but the lure of the professional game was strong, and the growing interest of Football League clubs from around the country was even stronger.

Southampton again expressed their interest and joining them were his favourites, Newcastle, their bitter local rivals, Sunderland, as well as York City, Blackpool, Huddersfield Town, little Lincoln City and from London, First Division Fulham. Newcastle was the obvious choice for such a devoted fan, but instead, and to everyone's surprise, he chose Fulham. This was solely due to the smooth-talking manager Bill Dodgin, the only manager who bothered to travel to the North East to talk to Bobby personally. Bill chatted to Bobby's mother and father and then sat in his car and waited for Bobby to emerge from his day at the pit.

Fulham had just won promotion to the top division and Dodgin persuaded Bobby that he would have a far greater chance of breaking into the first team with the Cottagers than he would with his local team, as Newcastle at that time were buying in big-name, ready-made stars.

It was a sound argument that won over Bobby, much to the surprise of his family, who fully expected him to join the squad at St James' Park. However, there was also great concern over Bobby's career as an electrician and it was only when he agreed to continue his apprenticeship in London that Philip finally agreed to his move south.

Bill Dodgin later confessed to being surprised at the conditions set by Mr and Mrs Robson, but he was so keen to capture the signature of this young wing-half that he readily agreed to the young Bobby Robson training in the evening with

Learning to live with success. Bobby (right) posing with brother Ron after raking in the awards for his local Langley Park team.

the part-timers instead of in the morning with the seniors. This reveals the sort of family the Robsons were: down-to-earth, solid Geordies. To them football was a game to be enjoyed and work was something else. Bobby did not argue as he followed a number of other youngsters from his Langley Park team to professional clubs. He was, however, the only one to make it all the way to the top. But it was a nervous and uncertain young man who packed his bags and left his village for the bright lights of London in 1950.

13

Bobby lived in digs within easy walking distance of the south London club, and shared with another young hopeful by the name of Tom Wilson. The two took to one another straightaway and undoubtedly helped each other to survive in this new, strange environment. It was, to say the least, a lasting friendship, as the two played together, were each other's best man at their respective weddings, and remain friends to this day.

"My father couldn't understand me when I went to Fulham, I think I disappointed him."

"I know the value of money. My father was a miner and had five kids."

Not the largest of players... Young Bobby sits 15
proudly clutching the club ball as captain of his
school football team, Waterhouses Modern
Intermediate. The teacher Mr David Gilliland
(back row, centre) encouraged Bobby greatly
and was his first mentor. Gilliland picked the
team and arranged matches for what was an
unofficial school team – considering the local
passion for the game it was amazing that there
wasn't an official team. Despite his size, Bobby
Robson quickly made his mark and led the
youngsters to a succession of victories,
establishing himself as one of the promising
young stars of the North East.

Bobby lines up with his successful Langley Park Junior team (*above*). Fortunately for Bobby (seated second from left), their games were a morning kick off to leave the pitch available for the adult team in the afternoon, thus allowing him to travel to Newcastle with his father, Philip, to watch his beloved United at St James' Park. This joyful marriage of playing and watching only survived until he was fifteen, when he was quickly promoted to the Under-18 side who kicked off in the afternoon.

A family day out by the seaside at Whitley Bay (*opposite*). Bobby (centre) and his brothers Ron and Thomas enjoy a holiday together.

2 **The London Alternative**

Because of his growing friendship with Tom Wilson and the easy-going attitude of manager Bill Dodgin, Bobby was to settle in at Craven Cottage and at his new digs. His lodgings featured something his North East home had not provided – hot running water, an indoor toilet and a bath.

Entertainment in London came from either the radio, the cinema or the theatre, with the two boys saving their money to go and watch the big stars of the time such as Sammy Davis Jr and even, on one memorable occasion, "Old Blue Eyes" himself, Frank Sinatra. They would stroll around Piccadilly Circus, people-watching and stopping for nothing more addictive or inebriating than a vanilla ice cream.

"When I was old enough to sign professionally, Newcastle came after me – and for some reason I chose Fulham."

The two young professional footballers took their training and fitness seriously, and decided that in order to progress they needed to eat properly. So, in addition to the huge breakfasts and evening meals which they received at their digs, they sometimes visited a local pub on Putney Bridge for a three-course lunch of soup, "meat and two veg" and a pudding with custard.

Despite enjoying his time in the capital, it was hardly a holiday, as Bobby, true to his word, found a job with an electrical company. One of his jobs took him to the Festival Hall, where his partner fell from the unfinished balcony to the concrete floor below, suffering multiple injuries. This made a lasting impression on the young Geordie, since it could so easily have been him who fell rather than his experienced colleague.

Bobby's working day as an electrician began at 6 am and did not finish until 7 pm, and three days a week he then went straight off to training at Craven Cottage. By the time Saturday came round the youngster was exhausted, and Bill Dodgin persuaded his parents to allow him to become a full-time professional footballer on the princely sum of £7 a week. This just about paid for his lodgings and food, as well as allowing him to save enough money to

Tasting the big time. A proud Bobby runs out onto the pitch at Craven Cottage, Fulham's home ground.

19

buy his parents a seven-day chiming clock, which he proudly presented to them at Christmas.

The summer break in those days was much longer for the league footballer than it is today and allowed Robson to go home, where he picked up £6 a week in wages. While in the North East he also played cricket, a game he had enjoyed since he was a child. He had a natural eye for the ball, and many of his friends and acquaintances believe that he could have made it in both sports – in those days many professional footballers were able to pursue football and cricket due to the long football close season.

Training full-time paid immediate and handsome dividends and Robson was able to miss out the apprentice professional side and all that entailed to step straight into full-time training with the first team. Meanwhile, Johnny Haynes, an apprentice and future England star, was still licking stamps in the club offices along with the other trainees Tosh Chamberlain, Tony Barton and Roy Dwight.

Bobby quickly became used to the roller coaster ride that is and always has been Fulham Football Club. In his first season in 1950–51 Fulham beat their wealthy neighbours Chelsea in the local derby in the fifth round of the FA Cup, drawing 1–1 at Stamford Bridge before thumping Chelsea 3–0 at the Cottage. But dreams of Wembley were quickly extinguished in the sixth round by the eventual winners, Newcastle.

"What is black and white and keeps going down?" asked Fulham chairman and comedian, Tommy Trinder, in his act. The answer was, of course, Fulham Football Club, as they were relegated again the next season. Because of the capped wages of the time (set to a limit of £14 in season and £12 in the summer) and the predictably large crowds, there was little financial change for the club between playing in the First and Second Division, only a change in prestige. No one at Fulham, in those days, was particularly bothered in a happy-go-lucky club which could draw 27,000 for almost every home match whatever division they were in. Players such as Bedford Jezzard, Charlie Mitten, Jim Taylor, the Lowe brothers (Reg and Eddie), Ian Black, Douggie Freeman and the rest simply shrugged and got on with the next season.

Robson stayed at Fulham until 1956, and the only surprise was that, with such talented players and such a large, supportive crowd, they did not go on to gain promotion and win honours. Apart from Robson, by now an England Under-23 and England B international, there were local legends such as Johnny Haynes, Jimmy Hill, Tom Wilson, Tony Macedo, Jimmy Langley and the ubiquitous Bobby Keetch. Tosh Chamberlain, Tony Macedo and Bobby Keetch, along with Charlie Mitten, who had been booted out of Old Trafford by Matt Busby, kept the dressing room in stitches with their zany humour.

"You have to have really strong will-power."

Robson, together with Johnny Haynes, who was recognized as one of the most creative midfield players not just in Britain but in the world, were a most formidable pairing. With that sort of energy coming from midfield it seems absurd that the club spent so much of the time that Robson played for them out of the top division. Perhaps there were just too many individualistic players and not enough of a team ethic in this fashionable London side who continually underachieved with the superb players that they had at their disposal.

There was always something happening at Craven Cottage and journalists could always find a story there with such characters as Jimmy Hill and Johnny Haynes. They certainly captured the headlines in later years when in 1961 Hill, in his role with the Professional Footballers' Association, campaigned to have the maximum wage scrapped. Players at the Cottage immediately benefited with England international Haynes becoming the first footballer to earn £100 a week.

Craven Cottage was clearly a fun place to play football but, already, Robson was looking and planning further ahead. As well as gaining international recognition he also took his first steps in the world of coaching, which was eventually to lead him to hold the position of England manager for eight years.

Jimmy Hill, who was to go on to become a successful manager with Coventry City from 1961 to 1967, and later a major television celebrity, was already a full badge coach and one of England manager Walter Winterbottom's favourite pupils. He was a loud, vocal presence, always ready to question the training methods and keen to implement ideas of his own.

Hill was not, however, as influential with Robson as another of the Fulham players. The centre half Ron Greenwood was an altogether quieter man, a deep thinker about the game and a man who was to help guide Robson into the world of coaching.

It was after watching England lose 6–3 and their unbeaten record at Wembley in November 1953 to Hungary that Robson decided to take the FA-run coaching courses at the earliest opportunity, following Greenwood and Hill.

"I don't think too many people know me that well..."

With so many deep-thinking footballers at the club, Robson was in his element, listening and contributing to the post-training session discussions, with Hill and Greenwood also offering their points of view. Robson eventually went on to succeed Greenwood as manager of England in June 1982, having helped him with his scouting at the World Cup in Spain.

Although Fulham were stuck outside the top division, Bobby was not unduly troubled as his international career continued to head in the right direction, including a close season tour in 1955 to the Caribbean, where an England team played against Trinidad, Jamaica, Bermuda and Curaçao. In the 1950s this was a massive and exotic undertaking, and it gave Robson a taste for the Caribbean which he was able to indulge later in his career, even taking Newcastle United to Trinidad and Tobago on an end-of-season tour.

On his return from the summer tour he married his childhood sweetheart Elsie, whom he had met at Langley Park some years earlier. They were wed in the local church where they lived, honeymooning first in Edinburgh before travelling to London, where they went boating on the River Thames. This nearly turned to disaster, as Elsie almost drowned while trying to fetch a pack of butter for the bank-side picnic. Struggling to stay afloat in the murky waters of the river, it was a life-and-death moment for the bride of just one week. Bobby pulled her out just in time before the heavy boat, which would have crushed her, swung back towards the bank.

Elsie was to repay the favour some years later when she forced her reluctant husband to go for a check-up on what he believed to be a simple nasal problem, but which turned out to be life-threatening cancer.

Life, then, was idyllic for Robson with his bride and a friendly club full of players he enjoyed working with. The only cloud on the horizon for this ambitious young man was the lack of motivation at this happy-go-lucky club. He was anxious to push ahead with his career and see how far he could go in the game.

With so many good quality players and such healthy crowds, it was remarkable that Fulham could not extricate themselves this time from the Second Division. So when West Bromwich Albion came in with a bid of £25,000 in 1956 for Robson's services – just £9,000 short of the British record – Fulham were in no position to refuse, even though Robson himself had had no thoughts of moving from the club he loved playing for.

While at Fulham Bobby Robson made 152 League appearances and scored a very respectable 69 goals from his attacking midfield role. It was one of the happiest times of his career and paved the way for his return as manager a number of years later.

"... the only real pal I ever had was a fellow called Tom Wilson. When I went to Fulham at seventeen years of age we shared a room together for about five years."

24

" When I first started at Craven
   Cottage there was a young
   man working in the office
   licking stamps. His name
   was Johnny Haynes."

Fulham's famous three (*above*). Bobby Robson (left), Bedford Jezzard (centre) and Johnny Haynes (right) relax at Craven Cottage following a training session.

Showing off to the cameras (*opposite*), Bobby (left) and Bedford (right) give a display of their impressive shooting skills. Fulham were, at the time, a team full of entertainers with individual brilliance. Never a championship challenging side, Fulham bobbed up and down between the top two divisions. This did not at all deter their loyal supporters, who enjoyed their flowing style of play and turned up in their thousands for every match.

A 1953 study of Fulham's young stars (*above*). Robson (front left), Jezzard (centre) and Haynes (right) lead the way in a relaxed training session, with a beardless Jimmy Hill (far left) following close behind. Hill later became a highly successful manager with Coventry City and a prominent television personality.

Robson, Jezzard and Haynes (*opposite*) descend the steps at Bobby's beloved Craven Cottage. Bobby was to return to the West London club twice, once as a player, and once as a manager.

Overleaf. Bobby began his professional career as an attacking wing-half, and was a regular on the score sheets. He is about to take the ball around Swansea City goalkeeper Edward Groves in 1953. This attempt was disallowed, robbing him of a hat trick.

3 Biking to the Baggies

Looking around the players' cars at Premier Division clubs these days is like viewing top-of-the-range automobiles at the most exclusive motor show. By contrast, after his massive £25,000 move to West Bromwich Albion in 1956, Bobby Robson's preferred mode of transport was his bicycle or his feet.

It was, of course, a different world. There was no five-star hotel for the expensive wing-half to move into when he arrived in the Midlands but, instead, more digs. A footballer's wage at that time meant, more often than not, that the player's wife continued to work to support their family. In this case, Elsie moved from her position at St Stephen's Hospital in London to the Deritend Stamping Company, where she was appointed industrial nurse. Financially, this was necessary, despite an increase in the professional footballer's wages from £14 a week in the winter and £12 in the summer to £20 and £18 respectively.

"You've got to be your own man, and if you aren't and you fail then you have no one to blame but yourself."

West Bromwich Albion, nicknamed the "Baggies" thanks to the voluminous shorts the team used to wear, was in the heart of the Black Country, so called for the most obvious reasons. Even the "Baggies" training ground was surrounded on three sides by heavy industry with chimneys belching black, acrid smoke, while on the other side was a canal, or "cut" as they called it in those parts. That canal was to play a significant role soon after Bobby left West Bromwich Albion. The manager of the time, Jimmy Hagan, not the most popular of men among his players because of his sharp tongue and strict discipline, let his car slip into the canal's murky waters. It was the players who had just felt the lash of their manager's abrasive tongue who saved his life.

In the famous stripes. West Bromwich Albion star, Bobby Robson, climbs high above the defence of Black Country rivals Wolverhampton Wanderers.

Fortunately for Bobby, when he arrived the manager was the smooth Vic Buckingham, a student of the Tottenham Hotspur push-and-run style developed under Arthur Rowe. Robson shared his beliefs in the way the game should be played, with one-touch football and everyone in the team involved.

Buckingham was the ideal boss to take his expensive young midfielder on to the next stage in his development. He had learned the lessons from the Hungarian disaster at Wembley and, what is more, had coached abroad in Holland with their top club Ajax, bringing back lots of fresh ideas, which impressed the budding coach in his ranks.

It also helped that Robson settled into his new surroundings with the minimum of effort. He loved the friendliness, wit and humour of the Black Country folk, who quickly made the Geordie feel welcome and at home.

He was also quick to find a new friend among the players – Don Howe. Just as with Tom Wilson at Fulham, the two quickly became firm friends and companions, a friendship that was to survive the years and the moves the two made, until they were gloriously reunited in 1982 when Bobby took over from Ron Greenwood as England manager. Bobby promptly made the shrewd and successful Howe – the moving force behind Arsenal's double triumph under Bertie Mee – his right-hand man in the England set-up and the two stayed together for the eight years. With great foresight Robson asked the entrenched Football Association to appoint Howe full time, but they claimed a lack of money stopped them, which was remarkable considering the dramatic excesses under the regime at the beginning of the twenty-first century.

Don Howe, as a player in 1956, was a smooth left back, and a sharp contrast to many of the shaven-headed, tough-tackling defenders of the day. The Hawthorns abounded with players who oozed real quality. Ronnie Allen, another player who went on successfully to manage abroad, was a centre forward who caressed the ball alongside the battering ram of Derek Kevan. There was Jimmy Dugdale, Jimmy Dudley and Maurice Setters. The team played football ahead of their time and were a joy to watch.

Established in both the club and the area, Bobby continued to make progress, becoming a full international in November 1957, despite the fierce competition

"We played beautiful football at West Brom and it provided me with the platform to gain recognition and earn my England call-up."

for his place from a list of quality players.

Bobby and Elsie had settled into the Midlands, buying a house in Handsworth, then a smart area of Birmingham, for £2,500. The solicitor who completed the conveyancing for the Robsons was West Bromwich Albion director Bert Millichip, later to become chairman of the Baggies and then Chairman of the Football Association, guiding them through their bleakest years of rampant football hooliganism. It was also Millichip who appointed Bobby Robson to manage England, revealing what a small world football can be.

Being naturally prudent, Robson was worried about borrowing too much money to buy the house in such an uncertain profession, but it did not affect his play or his progress. As well as becoming a full international in 1957 he was made skipper of his club team as they went in pursuit of the top honours, only to fail in the face of huge competition. At that time there were Matt Busby's "Babes" at Manchester United; local rivals Wolves under the stern control of Stan Cullis; a Spurs side heading towards their famous " Double" of League and FA Cup, plus the regular contenders from Arsenal, Aston Villa and, in those days, the superb footballing side of Burnley.

Despite now having a high profile, Bobby and his near neighbour David Burnside, without a car between them, would walk from Handsworth to the Hawthorns for training. This took at least half-an-hour, especially when the two would inter-pass and head a tennis ball between them along the way – a familiar sight for the boys from King Edwards and George Dixon Grammar Schools.

Even after the abrupt departure of Vic Buckingham, replaced by Gordon Clark, they were happy times. Robson, Howe, Allen and others would spurn the local snooker halls after training to sit in the nearby café talking about football and tactics. This formed the basis for their future development into coaching and management.

The future looked promising for the team and its content skipper, Robson, until in 1961 his old Fulham team-mate Jimmy Hill, now chairman of the PFA,

33

and the secretary Cliff Lloyd, helped to abolish the maximum wage after they were refused an increase from £20 a week to a more realistic £25.

His old team-mate Johnny Haynes soon became the first professional footballer on £100 per week, and Bobby Robson, as captain of West Bromwich Albion and a fully-fledged international player, naturally expected a similar increase to put him alongside the élite in the country. However, he was stunned to be told by the chairman Jim Gaunt that the club were offering him a measly rise to £25 per week and a bonus of £5 appearance money - cash he would not receive if he was injured or dropped.

Robson was disgusted at West Brom's reaction and promptly asked for a transfer. He was stripped of the captaincy by the manager Archie Macaulay, who gave the armband to his close friend, Don Howe, and Bobby was put on the transfer list in August 1962.

Robson didn't have to wait long to be sold, and it was his old club Fulham who headed the queue, stepping in just six years after selling him to West Brom, to buy him back for £20,000. He was delighted, even though his old club's situation had hardly changed from their roller coaster ride through the game. In the previous 1961–62 season Fulham had just missed out on a glamorous FA Cup final against Spurs when they lost to the Double-chasing Burnley team in the semi-finals, but in contrast they finished in twentieth place in the First Division, avoiding relegation by a single point.

The manager with the faith in Robson's experience and ability was none other than his old midfield partner Bedford Jezzard, who thought that his skilful former team-mate was the ideal choice to promote the exciting talent of his young midfield protégé, Alan Mullery. However, to everyone's dismay, the Board at Craven Cottage, without consulting Jezzard, sold the future England star to Spurs for £72,500 to help pay for the new stand they were building. Jezzard was so disappointed that it was not long before he resigned, and team affairs were taken over by Vic Buckingham, who had taken Bobby to West Brom in the first place.

The Baggies line-up before the start of the 1960–61 season. Bobby is sitting third from the left in the middle row, while his lifetime friend Don Howe is standing on the far right in the back row.

34

Buckingham fared little better than Jezzard and, before he had properly settled into his new position, he saw the next up-and-coming star, Rodney Marsh, sold to Queens Park Rangers – although this was partly compensated for when a thin young striker named Allan Clarke was signed from Walsall.

There was still an abundance of quality players at the Cottage, including Johnny Haynes, George Cohen, Eddie Lowe and the young Scot Graham Leggat. But had they retained the services of the likes of Mullery and Marsh, who knows what heights they may have scaled?

Robson stayed with Fulham until 1967 when whispers of a move to Arsenal disappeared and the offer of the job of player-manager at Southend did not appeal. In the end, he gave up the playing side of the game in England to move to Vancouver Royals in Canada in order to put together a side to play in the North American League.

Happy times at the Hawthorns. Individual squad photographs are taken by every club every season, and this one of Robson (*above*) is from his days at WBA. Bobby (*opposite*) flies through the air to avoid injuring Chelsea goalkeeper Reg Matthews at Stamford Bridge in 1957.

Previous pages. Robson comes to the rescue of his WBA goalkeeper, Jock Wallace, as he side-foots the ball to safety. Spurs, already League Champions, needed this win to break the total points record, but were denied by the Baggies, losing 2–1 on 1 May 1961.

4   The Young International

There is little doubt that playing for England shaped Bobby Robson's future as a coach and a manager and it was all due to one man – England coach Walter Winterbottom.

Mind you, had the difficulties faced by Winterbottom while he was England manager been there when Robson was offered the positon, Bobby would never have looked beyond club management.

It was, to be honest, farcical. The squad and the team were chosen by the International Committee, a group of chairmen from the League clubs who fought and squabbled over whom they should pick, reaching deals for their own players and then leaving their appointed coach to make the best of what they had given him. This strange state of affairs for one of the world's leading football countries remarkably did not change until Alf Ramsey was given complete charge after the World Cup in Chile and then went on to win the 1966 World Cup at Wembley.

"The International Committee picked the team and then passed on the names for Walter Winterbottom to lick into shape."

A classic example of the inequitable system was shown following Robson's debut against France in 1957, with a team line-up of Eddie Hopkinson, Don Howe, Roger Byrne, Ron Clayton, Billy Wright, Duncan Edwards, Bryan Douglas, Tommy Taylor, Johnny Haynes and Tom Finney. From his attacking midfield role Robson scored twice in a four-goal victory at Wembley, but was then promptly dropped for the next game against Scotland. The player who replaced him was a little-known youngster from Manchester United called Bobby Charlton. Charlton scored on his debut and England again won 4–0.

Robson, however, went on to win another nineteen caps, scoring two more goals for England, and was involved in both the 1958 and the 1962 World Cup Finals. England, unfortunately, failed on both occasions to make the impact that the quality of their players suggested they might.

Training hard.
Bobby Robson (right) and Johnny Haynes "do the wheelbarrow" while training for the 1958 World Cup Finals in Gothenburg, Sweden.

41

Robson was in his element in that very first game against France, playing alongside "Busby Babes" he had long admired, such as Tommy Taylor and Roger Byrne, not to mention the outstanding newcomer, Dudley-born and Manchester United-bred, Duncan Edwards. Tragically, Bobby's first game for England with them was their last together, for, four months later, they were killed in the 1958 Munich Air Disaster on their way back from a European Cup tie in Yugoslavia.

Bobby felt the loss of the brilliant, young Edwards more than most, for the supporters of West Bromwich Albion considered him one of their own, even though he played at Old Trafford. Edwards was their "local boy made good" and they believed he was destined to become a great English footballer.

With the loss of so many quality players, along with the strange way that the squad and team were selected, it was a frustrating time for everyone concerned with English football.

Another classic example of the inequitable system was in the 1958 World Cup Finals in Sweden, when the Football Association arbitrarily cut the squad from twenty-two to twenty. This was bad enough in itself, but the two players that they left out were Stanley Matthews and Nat Lofthouse. It wasn't even because they were too old. Nat Lofthouse, "The Lion of Vienna", had just scored two goals for Bolton Wanderers to beat Manchester United in the Cup Final at Wembley, while Stan had a great deal left to offer, as he showed four years later when he ran the legendary Brazilian Nilton Santos ragged at Wembley.

Robson remembers with regret how Tom Finney was injured in the first game in the World Cup Finals against the Soviet Union (and did not play again), while Robson himself had a goal inexplicably disallowed in the same game; a goal that would have won the match for England.

More disappointment was to follow when neither Pele nor Garrincha played for Brazil in the next game England faced, although Robson hardly had time to notice as he tracked Didi and Dino in a 0–0 draw. That left England needing to beat Austria in the final group game, and again Robson had a perfectly good goal disallowed in a 2–2 draw. A play-off against the Soviet Union was the result. Robson was axed by the committee, who brought in Wolves' player Peter Broadbent, and England were packed off home early by a goal from Ilyin.

Despite the disappointment, Robson fell in love with the competition. The World Cup had suddenly become the pinnacle for him, and he immediately set his sights on making up for the disappointments of Sweden by targeting Chile four years later.

> **"We beat Scotland 9–3.**
> **That was fabulous.**
> **A historical game and**
> **I scored the first goal**
> **that day."**

Robson became a regular member of the England team and during one outstanding spell between October 1960 and May 1961 he played in a remarkable sequence of matches which saw England win six successive games and score a staggering forty goals on the way. This included the memorable 9–3 victory over Scotland at Wembley, when Robson opened the scoring in what is England's biggest ever win over Scotland.

By the time the World Cup Finals in Chile came round Bobby was recognized as a more defensive wing-half and was first choice as the squad prepared to make their way out to South America. He played in the final game before departure in a 3–1 win against Switzerland at Wembley, but then gave way to the youngster Bobby Moore, so he could gain experience in a friendly in Peru. Robson then agonizingly cracked his ankle-bone in training on arrival in Chile, which signified not only the end of his World Cup but also his international career. He did not play again for England, while his replacement, Moore, went on to win over 100 caps, captain his country and lift the World Cup.

Bobby Robson had to watch that World Cup from the sidelines, but with team-mates such as Bobby Charlton, Bryan Douglas, Ray Wilson, Gerry Hitchens, Jimmy Greaves, his old Fulham team-mate Johnny Haynes, Maurice

Norman, Ron Flowers, Ron Springett, Jimmy Armfield and Bobby Moore, England hoped to go all the way this time.

Although Robson worked hard on his fitness and would have been ready for the semi-final, a 3–1 defeat by Brazil in the quarter-final signalled the end of England's hopes.

Robson continued to move further back on the pitch, now playing in defence for Fulham, and by the time of the 1966 World Cup Finals he was playing alongside the centre half. He hoped for an England recall, but Alf Ramsey, the man he was to follow as both Ipswich and England manager, thought otherwise. There was no way back.

44   The World Cup did, however, shape his future career. It was during the 1953 tournament that Winterbottom approached both Robson and his England room-mate Don Howe, asking them what they planned to do with their futures. He persuaded them to seriously consider coaching, and to take their preliminary coaching badges at Lilleshall, the FA training headquarters. Robson had qualified for his full badge by the time the team travelled out to Chile four years later and on his return FA coach Alan Wade asked him if he wanted some coaching work. With a growing family and a house in Worcester Park, he quickly agreed.

Vic Buckingham, Bobby's manager at Fulham, actively encouraged him and even gave him time off to coach the Oxford University team. Bobby travelled 240 miles a week for £2 a training session, and there were instant rewards as Oxford beat their great rivals Cambridge in two successive Varsity matches after a long run of defeats.

Robson also became a staff coach for the Surrey Football Coaches Association, coaching the coaches, lecturing and assessing would-be coaches and even coaching the Pearl Assurance Football team as a favour to a friend. This he did twice a week and was rewarded with a fee that was three shillings above the accepted £2.25 rate.

Young Lions.
Bobby (left) and his Fulham and England team-mate Johnny Haynes at Craven Cottage.

"I cracked my ankle-bone on the way out to the 1962 World Cup and lost my place to a young whippersnapper named Bobby Moore."

Full of hope and expectation. The England squad (*above*) line up before leaving for the 1962 World Cup Finals in Chile. They would have to wait another four years for their first and only success in the competition. Bobby Robson (back row third from left) started off as a first-choice player, but suffered injury and gave way to a young Bobby Moore (standing far right), who went on to lead England to success at Wembley in 1966.

Previous pages. Tom Finney, watched by Bobby, gives England hope in the 1958 World Cup Finals with a penalty to level the scores at 2–2 against Russia in Gothenburg on 8 June 1958. It was to no avail, however, as England were eliminated from the tournament.

Always one to watch as many matches as he could. Bobby
and other members of the England squad (*above*) stand to
attention for the national anthems before watching Argentina in
a goalless draw with Hungary in Rancagua in the 1962 World
Cup Finals in Chile. Left to right: George Eastham, Don Howe,
Ron Flowers, Bobby Robson and Harold Shepherdson.

England's brilliant young defender Bobby Moore (*opposite*),
who replaced the injured Robson, is pictured in the thick of the
action against defending champions Brazil in the 3–1 defeat at
Viña del Mar, Chile 1962.

5   Back at the Cottage

Bobby Robson reached another milestone in 1967, when at the age of thirty-four he bought his first car, a Morris Minor. Realizing that his playing career was drawing to a close, he turned his thoughts to the next stage in his footballing life – either coaching or managing.

Armed with his coaching certificates and badges and the experiences with Oxford University and other amateur clubs, he sought a new challenge.

The first offer he got was from Southend, two divisions lower than Fulham, and Robson followed it up by agreeing to meet one of his cricketing heroes, Trevor Bailey of Essex and England, at the time a director at the southeast Essex club. Robson was not keen on dropping as low as the Third Division, even for his first job, and when he heard that the salary on offer was considerably less than the £3,500 a year he was picking up at Craven Cottage, the job at Southend was never a serious consideration.

" I had a few trials and tribulations and a few ups and downs."

Arsenal had also shown an interest behind the scenes and Robson desperately hoped for a concrete follow-up, but it never reached the stage of a full approach.

Bobby had decided that there were still a few miles left in his legs and turned his attention to becoming a player-coach. An opportunity arose almost immediately when the newly formed Vancouver Royals made him an offer. After long discussions with Elsie about the schooling of their three sons, Paul Martin, Andrew Peter and Robert Mark, they set sail on the *SS Oriana* for a new life in Canada.

The return. Bobby, now back with Fulham, holds off the firm and determined challenge of Sheffield United's Alan Woodward in this First Division clash in February 1967.

The cruise – instead of a flight – was taken deliberately so that the family could enjoy a long, leisurely holiday for three weeks as Bobby looked forward to a job, that had, in a stroke, doubled his wages. The prospect of such an increase in income encouraged the Robson family to travel first class with stops at exotic places such as Bermuda, Port Everglades, the Panama Canal, Los Angeles and San Francisco.

53

There were no fears, either, of Vancouver, a city he had fallen in love with on an end-of-season tour with West Bromwich Albion. He felt he had fallen on his feet.

But the great promise evaporated before his eyes, with the club hitting serious financial problems, with no players and no pay. Robson felt terrible because he had spent weeks recruiting players from around the world, including two from Hong Kong to represent the growing Chinese population in the city.

Eventually, the club found a new backer by merging with another start-up club, but the accountants insisted on bringing in Ferenc Puskas, the legendary

A last-ditch challenge. Bobby slides in to deny Blackpool a cross.

Hungarian inside forward, and the arrangements became ever more chaotic, while the money owed to Robson grew even larger.

A major legal battle threatened, until Fulham Secretary Graham Hortop stepped in and offered Bobby a chance to return to Craven Cottage. His decision to take the job, against the advice of his legal team, was vindicated when the Canadian club folded after just four months, while still owing everyone involved a great deal of money.

It all looked rosy at Fulham, with the Chairman Tommy Trinder now backed by the financial muscle of the wealthy Sir Eric Miller, even though, when Bobby arrived in January, the club was already involved in yet another relegation struggle and were on their way down to the Second Division once more. With the prospect of glory receding, there was suddenly little money available to improve the squad, and within nine months Bobby was out of work again after reading about it on an *Evening Standard* billboard on his way home from work.

That November morning in the office Robson had received a call from a journalist and ex-Arsenal footballer Bernard Joy asking him if anything was happening at the club. A perplexed Robson knew nothing of any impending changes at Craven Cottage and approached Hortop, who claimed he knew nothing either. But after reading the *Evening Standard* headline and story Robson immediately contacted directors Chappie D'Amato and the Dean family, only to be met by embarrassed silence before it was admitted that it was Miller who had sacked him that very morning without thought or discussion. When they finally met, Robson was simply told that the results were not good enough and he had to go.

A tearful Robson stood alone on the centre circle at the ground he had graced so often, shed a few tears of regret and vowed never to return.

After the Canadian experience as well it was a shattering blow to a young man with his foot on the first steps of the managerial ladder. He had signed a three-year contract with Fulham and had been working hard to change the fortunes of the club he knew and loved.

55

This devastating blow was dealt by the man who had sold Alan Mullery to have a stand built and named after him and who, when the pressure grew, committed suicide. Miller's death gave Robson no pleasure at all.

Before his abrupt dismissal Robson had arranged for the transfer of goalscorer Allan Clarke to Leicester City for cash with a strong centre forward named Frank Large in return, while another deal had seen him sign a local youngster from Tonbridge for £1,000. Malcolm Macdonald was a left back at the time but went on to ever-greater things as a centre forward with Newcastle, Arsenal and England.

Bobby's sacking came just as he was finding his feet and he was hardly consoled by the old adage in football that you could never become a truly great manager until you had been sacked at least once. It was also a problem because the Robson family, backed by the three-year contract, had bought a house in the Surrey stockbroker belt and their three boys had entered private schools. Bobby decided to live off his savings until they dwindled to such a low point that he was forced to join the dole queue, where, to his surprise, he found it full of businessmen and even a retired army major rather than the scroungers he had expected to encounter.

It was little satisfaction that Miller had appointed Robson's old mate Johnny Haynes to replace him. Johnny hated the job and the interference and lasted only a month before quitting. He was replaced by Bill Dodgin Jr, who was unable to save the club from plummeting into the Third Division as Miller continued his interference with everything from buying and selling players to team selection.

This was a bleak time for the ambitious young manager and, not having had a single game in charge in Canada and just ten month's experience, including a close season at Fulham, he had little to offer as references for a needy club. Then Dave Sexton came to his rescue when he asked him to do some scouting for Chelsea. The very first match he was asked to attend was between Ipswich Town and Nottingham Forest at Portman Road, two clubs who had both recently parted company with their managers. At first Robson thought he would reject the chance to go to the game in case it looked as though he was touting for either job, but in the end he went – and applied for both.

Forest did not even bother to reply to his letter and minimal CV, but Ipswich, searching for a successor to Bill McGarry, who had quit after four years, invited Robson to Portman Road to discuss the job. He was well aware of their reputation for looking after their managers, and they also had a background of success after Alf Ramsey had led them to the First Division title in 1962 before leaving to take over the England job.

"I was told to report to the board and they told me they were dispensing with my services. I walked to the middle of Craven Cottage, to the centre circle, it was absolutely deserted. I shed tears."

According to the bookmakers, Robson was a rank outsider, trailing a long way behind the favourites Frank O'Farrell and Billy Bingham. Frank, who was to go on to manage Manchester United, and Billy, who enjoyed such success with Everton before taking over at the helm of Northern Ireland, both declined, with Frank deciding to stay with Torquay and Billy not wanting to leave his job unfinished at Plymouth.

Suddenly, a job which had so many obstacles in front of it had opened up for a new contender. So in January 1969, Bobby Robson met the chairman John Cobbold, along with Harold Smith and Ken Brightwell, in the Great Western Hotel in London. There, after a relaxed and pleasant interview, they offered him the job of manager of Ipswich Town, but without the security of a contract.

Although he was told it meant at least two years with the club, he had his doubts over such a commitment after his recent experiences, even at a salary of around £5,000 a year, but after leaving the room to think about it he quickly returned, shook hands and began a new adventure.

Two totally committed players (*above*). Bobby (left) scrambles the ball clear from the arch predator Denis Law as the Scot closes in, in a clash with Manchester United at Craven Cottage on 26 March 1967.

In the same game (*opposite*) Robson (4) comes to the rescue as Fulham desperately defend against Manchester United in the pulsating 2–2 draw. World Cup star George Cohen is on the line just in case, while John Dempsey (5) is out of action on the floor as Bill Foulkes (5) and David Sadler (9) press for the winning goal.

"I had a three-year contract at Fulham and lasted eight months. I was bitter about it and wondered if I would ever get another chance?"

Calm experience and youthful exuberance (*below*). Bobby (left) trains alongside a young Allan Clarke in November 1966. Bobby was by now beginning to think about his future, while his young colleague, known as "Sniffer", was a predator of the first order. Clarke eventually moved on to Leeds United, where, under another future England manager, Don Revie, he went on to win many honours and earn a regular place in the England side.

Robson (*opposite*) enjoying the thrill of his first managerial position at Fulham in 1968.

6 The Champagne Years

Bobby Robson's record at Ipswich marks him as one of the outstanding managers of his era, even before his adventures at international level and on the Continent. Yet it did not start off that way. At any other club he might have found himself out of work for a third time and with little or no chance of a return to the business he has now graced for more than thirty-five years.

The first two years were a genuine struggle as he clashed with players, suffered bad results and was targeted by the irate supporters, who chanted "Robson Out, Robson Out" as an upcoming Irishman named George Best turned his side inside-out with a stunning hat trick. A board meeting was called for the day after that match and Robson feared the worst, only to have the Ipswich Town chairman John Cobbold apologise for the fans' awful behaviour and then give him £70,000 to spend on Blackburn Rovers' centre half Allan Hunter.

"I was a young manager. I had no reputation. I had no credibility. I had no CV. I wondered who was going to employ me?"

Robson loved working for the Cobbold brothers John and Patrick, famously recalling their only moment of crisis when the Sancerre ran out in the boardroom. When they clinched a big sponsorship deal John solemnly declared, "It has been suggested that we will squander the money on wine, women and song. That is absolute nonsense. We don't do a lot of singing at Portman Road."

It was an environment in which Bobby Robson flourished. He was not only coach and manager but he did nearly everything else concerning the team, all except sweep the dressing room floor.

Robson went on to build three top teams at Portman Road, winning the FA Cup Final in 1978, the UEFA Cup in 1981 and two successive Youth Cups in 1974 and 1975. During his time as manager, Ipswich were regularly in the top three league teams, ensuring ongoing qualification for European competitions. This was quite an achievement considering the size of the East Anglian club, who

Happy days.
Robson enjoys a joke as Ipswich manager.

"I went on the dole. I didn't know what else to do because I had no money. Six months later I had a job at Ipswich on six thousand pounds a year."

were competing with clubs including Liverpool, Leeds and Manchester United. Robson even helped to rebuild the team's ground, Portman Road, by refusing to spend all of the club's money on players.

Robson had to earn the right to manage at the club he was to make his own. As a raw, inexperienced boss with nothing to show for his brief ventures into management, he was challenged by some of the senior professionals at Portman Road when he tried to establish his position. Tommy Carroll and Bill Baxter tested his authority to the limits until the Irishman Carroll made an aggressive move by ripping down the teamsheet which he had been omitted from. Robson swung into action and a wrestle ensued; the Scot Baxter then joined in with Robson fighting for his managerial life. Once again the board backed him and neither player played for the club again, with Carroll signing for Birmingham and Baxter going to Hull for a combined total of £31,000. Robson had been told he could give them away, but he wisely preferred to wait, sell them and have the money.

Robson worked hard to transform his team's fortunes and to change the side around, but he is the first to credit his scouts for spotting the talent that went on to form the basis for his successful Ipswich sides. Ray Tyrell brought in local youngsters like Brian Talbot, Trevor Whymark, Mick Lambert, Clive Woods, Roger Osborne and Mick Mills. When Tyrell left, his successor George Finlay discovered John Wark, Alan Brazil and George Burley from Glasgow, while John Carruthers spotted Kevin Beattie, Eric Gates, David Geddes and Robin Turner. Bobby's brother Tom also weighed in with Russell Osman, who, in partnership with Terry Butcher, formed the rock on which the Ipswich defence was formed. Robson himself turned away a rather plump little player, Paul Gascoigne.

Robson also dipped into the transfer market, never going higher than the £70,000 he paid for Hunter in those early days, but he brought in Frank Clark, David Johnson, Jimmy Robertson and goalkeeper Paul Cooper.

A club of that size needed to keep things turning over to remain in the upper echelons and in order to buy Bobby also had to sell. The club picked up huge fees for the likes of Brian Talbot, who went to Arsenal, and David Geddes, who continued his career at Aston Villa.

Robson's success on a limited budget had other clubs looking anxiously towards Portman Road wondering what it would take to prise this man away. Everton, for one, made several attempts over the years to lure him to Goodison Park, while Derby County approached him to replace the hugely successful Brian Clough, and Leeds United wanted him when Don Revie left to manage England.

It wasn't just clubs from England. Football was breaking down the borders, as Robson himself showed in the 1978–79 season, when he organized the revolutionary signings of Dutchmen Frans Thijssen and Arnold Muhren. Barcelona over the years made three attempts to lure him to Spain with the promise of good remuneration, as did Bilbao, the Basque club, who liked the idea of an English manager after being founded by English ex-patriots.

Sunderland almost lured Robson back to his home territory when they offered to double his salary to do for them what he had done for Ipswich. At the other end of the scale, Manchester United approached him in May 1981 to succeed Dave Sexton. The chairman Martin Edwards called to offer him the job as Ipswich celebrated their UEFA Cup victory in Amsterdam after beating AZ 67 Alkmaar of Holland 5–4 on aggregate. But again Robson said no, and they turned instead to Ron Atkinson at West Bromwich Albion, who gave them an immediate yes.

Robson turned down the glory because he believed it was due at Portman Road. He had built several fine sides who constantly went close to winning the one trophy that had eluded him, and which he desired most of all: the League Championship. Ipswich flirted with the top places, twice finishing runners-up to Aston Villa and Liverpool as their squads proved just a touch too weak. His argument was that with their finances they could not afford top wages sitting on the bench.

There was the occasional hitch, such as when they finished three points off relegation in 1977–78, but, in the same season, they reached Wembley where they

"When I look back at when I stood on the ground at Craven Cottage when I had the sack I vowed then that I would never be in that position again. So when I met the problem, I dealt with it."

were considered by the bookmakers as 5–2 no-hopers against the mighty Arsenal.

The FA Cup is very special to the traditionalist Robson, so this final in 1978 was one of the great days of his life, as unheralded Roger Osborne scored the winning goal, famously collapsing shortly afterwards with the emotion of it all. Not only did Ipswich win the Cup, but they were undoubtedly the better team.

That Cup was the most treasured, cherished and polished trophy in the history of the game, stored in a bank vault every night except when it was hidden under Robson's bed at his home in Ipswich. It was returned to the Football Association in better condition than when Ipswich had received it!

But Robson knew that the FA Cup Final had only covered up the cracks, and this was proved when Nottingham Forest humbled Ipswich 5–0 in the Charity Shield. He promptly went on the offensive and bought Arnold Muhren for £150,000 and Frans Thijssen for £220,000 – £80,000 less than Arsenal had paid for Brian Talbot. Come the 1980–81 season Ipswich were back chasing the glory.

With youngsters like Butcher, Osman and Brazil coming through the ranks, Ipswich and Robson rekindled the flame and enjoyed another tremendous season, beating the eventual League champions Aston Villa three times. However, they lost to Manchester City in the FA Cup semi-final and then contrived to throw away the title, which seemed to be theirs, with the end of the season in sight. The only team they beat in a spell of five games was, incredibly, Manchester City.

But while they slipped at the final hurdles in the 1980–81 season, they galloped away in Europe as they put out Aris Salonika, Bohemians Prague, Widzew Lodz (conquerors of Manchester United in the previous round) and the talented St Etienne (whose stars included Platini, Battiston, Larios and Castenada), in the quarter-finals of the UEFA Cup with a 4–1 win in France, the first time St Etienne had lost a home European tie for twenty-six years.

Ipswich dispatched a Cologne side in the semi-final, which included another host of Internationals, with Schumacher, Zimmermann, Bonhof, Konopka, Muller, Engels and England International Tony Woodcock.

66

Ready for the new season. The Ipswich Town squad line-up in July 1975. They are (back row, left to right) Robson, Peddelty, Talbot, Whymark, Cooper, Sivall, Hunter, Burley, Beattie and Lee. (Front row, left to right) Lambert, Osborne, Mills, Hamilton, Johnson, Woods, Gates, Harper.

Prior to the semi-final, Ipswich were forced to play a gruelling fixture list, with Arsenal at home on the Saturday, local derby rivals Norwich City on Monday, Cologne on Wednesday and Manchester City on Saturday. No wonder the Germans laughed, but it was cut short when Ipswich won 1–0 again in Germany.

Just when it looked as though the promising season would yield nothing, Ipswich grabbed the UEFA Cup, a competition that had featured not only Manchester United and St Etienne but also Juventus and Barcelona. In the final, Ipswich won 3–0 at home against AZ 67 Alkmaar and then clinched the trophy, despite losing the second leg 4–2. It was a continual, wonderful roller coaster ride

68

"When we won John Cobbold had a bottle of champagne and when we lost he had two bottles of champagne. That was his civilized way of looking at defeat. He was a remarkable guy, an outstanding fellow."

Never a dull moment. John (*opposite*, *left*) and Patrick Cobbold (*opposite*, *right*), the owners of Ipswich Town, who gave Bobby his second chance as a manager. He could not have found better, for both the brothers, and John in particular, were full of fun, backing him all the way even when the club was struggling. The atmosphere from the boardroom spilled over into the dressing room in what was a very happy club.

There was always a sense of fun at Portman Road (*above*), with Bobby Robson scratching his head and wondering what is going to happen next with two of his more unpredictable Ipswich Town players David Johnson (left) and Bobby's greatest English discovery Kevin Beattie (right). Both went on to play for England but, while Beattie remained with Ipswich, Johnson moved on to join the all-conquering Liverpool side, where he enjoyed success at home and in Europe, scoring eight goals in fifteen games.

Following in the footsteps. Bobby succeeded Sir Alf Ramsey (*above*) not only as manager of Ipswich Town but also as manager of England. Ramsey and Robson are still Ipswich's and England's most successful managers, and both legends have their statues outside Ipswich's ground today.

Bobby (*opposite and overleaf*) doing what he likes most: getting close to his players, improving their skills and sorting out the tactics for the next game.

"I had a great quality of life. Nobody had a better car than me, and nobody earned more money than me. I was the best-paid person at Ipswich and the chairman would not let players earn more than me. That doesn't happen now."

"On the sidelines... you often see a chance building in the

attack... to break through... which players sometimes don't!"

"The right club came in for me at the right time. I finished up with a ten-year contract. I finally finished working there after fourteen years."

74

The taste of success. In the 1978 FA Cup Final at Wembley, Arsenal were odds on favourites to bury the "Tractor Boys" from Ipswich, but Robson found the most unlikely hero when the unheralded Roger Osborne scored a deserved winning goal (*above*). It was all too much for the player as the emotion of the moment drained the last reserves of his energy, and he played no further part in the 1–0 victory.

A well-deserved celebration in the changing rooms after Ipswich's suprising win (*opposite*).

A moment to savour (*left*). The dream 77 had become a reality. Ipswich had won the FA Cup against all the odds, beating the mighty Arsenal by just 1–0 but winning the game by a distance. Mick Mills and Brian Talbot have a firm grip on the cup, while Clive Woods looks ready to take the base home.

The entire town of Ipswich turned out to welcome home the conquering heroes and famous trophy (*above*).

"It was a matter of personal pride to keep Ipswich in the black and to play good, attractive football."

78   **A safe pair of hands.** One of the reasons for Ipswich Town's success under Bobby Robson was the goal-defying performances of goalkeeper Paul Cooper. He was not the biggest of goalkeepers, but he was extremely agile and made a speciality of saving penalties in the days when the keeper had to stay rooted to the line until the ball was struck. He gave his defence great confidence with his consistent, high-grade performances. His best efforts were not always good enough though, as a shot from another master, Liverpool and Scotland's Kenny Dalglish, flies past him in a 2–0 defeat in March 1979.

It will be all right in the end. Robson and his Ipswich assistant, Bobby Ferguson, look decidedly unimpressed (above) as they squirm on the bench in April 1981 watching Ipswich battle with FC Cologne in the second leg of the UEFA Cup semi-final. There was no need to worry, though, as Ipswich had done enough in the first leg (winning 1–0) to reach the final.

Ipswich and England striker Paul Mariner (*opposite*) shows his feelings after the 2–1 win against fellow title challengers and League leaders Aston Villa. This closed the gap at the top of the First Division to a single point, and Ipswich had a game in hand on Villa.

Overleaf. This is what it means to Bobby to win a big game. His centre half, Terry Butcher, had just scored a 64th-minute goal to give Ipswich a two-goal aggregate lead against FC Cologne in the semi-final of the 1981 UEFA Cup.

84

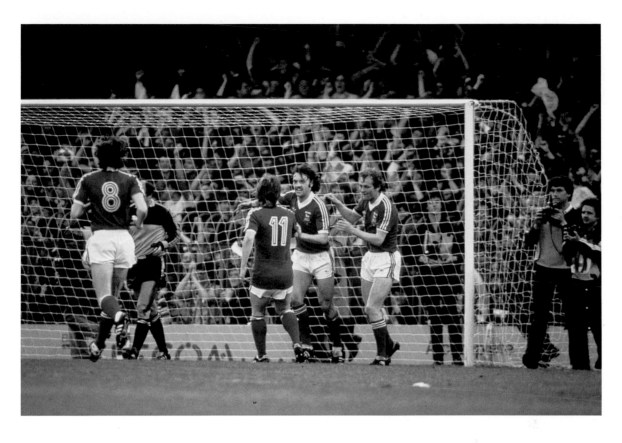

"I have always tried to spend the club's money as if it were my own."

Going Dutch in a big way (*opposite*). Bobby tries on a clog with his two top Dutch signings, Frans Thijssen (left) and Arnold Muhren (right), before the second leg of the UEFA Cup Final against Alkmaar 67 in Holland. Robson heralded the mass arrival of foreign players with his astute signings of these two quality players, who took Ipswich to a new, more refined level. It opened the gates for other managers to start scouring the world to bring in the best to improve their teams and, eventually, the level of football played throughout the country.

It was a homegrown Scot, John Wark (*above*), who celebrated scoring the first goal in the first leg of the UEFA Cup Final against Alkmaar 67 at Portman Road in 1981. Ipswich went on to win 3–0.

Success in Europe. Frans Thijssen (*above*) wheels away in
triumph having scored for Ipswich in the second leg of their
UEFA Cup Final against Alkmaar 67. Ipswich lost a thrilling
second leg 4–2, but 5–4 on aggregate was enough to see
Bobby Robson win his first ever European trophy.

Bobby lifts the cup in triumph (*opposite*) in Princes Street,
Ipswich, as the team and the town celebrate the outsiders
winning yet again against all the odds. So great were the
manager's sentimental ties to the club that it was only in the
summer of 2003 that he eventually sold his home in Ipswich
after losing his precious England caps in a burglary.

"He would really accentuate the positives and accentuate what you were good at... I get hairs on the back of my neck standing up now, thinking of the times when he's brought me back to his office and said these things."

TERRY BUTCHER

Seeing the funny side. Robson raises a smile as his skipper, Terry Butcher (left), and assistant, Bobby Ferguson (right), argue the point. It was a successful combination; Ferguson took over at Ipswich when Bobby moved on to manage England; while Terry, an England hero in every sense of the word, went on to manage teams in England and Scotland, as well as carving out a successful career as a radio broadcaster. Butcher was a key figure at Portman Road under Robson, and later with him at international level.

89

A career cut short. Of all the players Bobby Robson had at
Ipswich, it was Kevin Beattie whom he rated above all others. But
like another Northern boy, Paul Gascoigne, Kevin got himself into
all sorts of scrapes at home and on the pitch, until an injury cruelly
brought his outstanding career to a shuddering close. Beattie (above)
shows the raw power and strength that made him such a feared
defender at domestic and international level.

You can see the pride and sorrow on the face of Bobby Robson
(*opposite*) as he watches Kevin Beattie take the plaudits of the
Portman Road crowd as he leaves the field in the second half of the
2–2 draw with Moscow Dynamo in Beattie's testimonial game in
March 1982. Robson missed his player at both club and
international level.

"When I was manager at Ipswich I used to come up and steal players from Newcastle, including Paul Gascoigne, he was very wide and he was clever. But I never signed him."

"I have had difficult times. I have won this and won that but I have also had it rough, and you do not get to the top unless it has been rough at some stage."

92

Pure enthusiasm. Passion has always been a strong point in Bobby Robson, as evident before, during and after matches – and not just the big ones. He made himself known to most of the top referees and linesmen during his long career, but saved himself from punishment and banishment to the stands by being polite and respectful, no matter what the circumstances. Bobby (*opposite*) is expressing his opinion about Leeds United's time-wasting tactics back in late September 1981. Despite his concerns Ipswich went on to win 2–1.

Overleaf. Sometimes, however, it doesn't go your way and the upsets come from the most unexpected sources. This time it is little Shrewsbury Town putting one over on Bobby Robson's Ipswich Town in the fifth round of the FA Cup in February 1982. Bobby seems to be able to see it coming as Bobby Ferguson points out the latest deficiency.

"I don't think my family have suffered but they haven't seen enough of me and I haven't seen enough of them. I didn't spend enough time with my three sons because the job was eating at me and I regret that."

97

Part of the game is losing, and losing gracefully.
This time (*opposite*) it's a handshake and a word of congratulations to his close friend and Notts County manager Howard Wilkinson in January 1982, as they follow off Kevin O'Callaghan after a shock 3–1 home defeat.

It's not what you say, but the way that you say it (*above*). Robson talks to the press on a much happier day.

"One of the biggest decisions I have ever taken in my

98 **Parting is such sweet sorrow.** Bobby Robson says his farewells to skipper Mick Mills and the rest of the Ipswich team as he leaves in August 1982 to take on the England job.

life was that *decision, to leave Ipswich and go to England."*

7 The Best Job in the World

On his own admission it took Bobby Robson at least two years to settle into the England job, so different was it to club management.

No manager of England, before or since, has suffered the way Robson did in his eight years at Lancaster Gate with the Football Association. The problem was that he found himself in the middle of a tabloid circulation war, which exposed his personal life and laid him open to fierce and unfair criticism, whether it was regarding a friendly warm-up international or a World Cup game.

The constant carping and criticism, ten times that aimed at subsequent bosses Sven Goran Eriksson, Glenn Hoddle, Graham Taylor or Kevin Keegan, even turned the fans against him. Spectators at Wembley spat at him as he walked head bowed towards the dressing room after a defeat, and he was vilified by his own beloved Newcastle fans after he left Kevin Keegan out of his first England squad.

"...as well as a manager he is also a gentleman and a human being."

FRANZ BECKENBAUER

Few would have suffered the abuse the way Robson did. They would have run for the hills or, at least, taken up one of the offers from clubs like Barcelona who tried to persuade him he did not need to take the criticism hurled at him through the media.

Robson not only stuck it out but took England to the quarter-finals of the World Cup in Mexico in 1986, where England were beaten by the "Hand of God" goal and another moment of inspiration by Diego Maradona. Four years later he took England to the semi-finals of the competition, losing only to the eventual winners West Germany in a harrowing penalty shoot-out.

To this day only Sir Alf Ramsey, another former Ipswich boss, has taken England further, and no manager has ever taken England as far in World Cup competitions away from these shores.

Reason to be cheerful. Bobby takes on the job of his dreams as manager of England.

What is also conveniently forgotten is that Robson was not only fighting the tabloid press but also the even more damaging hooligan element that infested the game while he was in charge. Imagine the feeling in Mexico the year before the

World Cup Finals when England were due to face Italy only hours after the death and destruction of the European Cup Final between Liverpool and Juventus in Brussels.

After that, English clubs were banned from Europe, depriving Robson's top players of invaluable experience against the world's best players. In those days the majority of the players in the First Division were from the home nations with only the odd import. Because of the hooligan threat the FA also had to be careful where and who they played in warm-up internationals. It was akin to asking England to play all their matches with only one boot per player.

The fact that it was a near impossible situation for an international manager was shown when English clubs were finally allowed back into European competitions. Their previous levels of success in all three tournaments, especially the European Cup, took several years to restore.

The great irony is that Bobby's remarkable success at international level has only recently been recognized, as a succession of new managers have faced the realities of international football without having to carry the burden of hooliganism and suspension on their backs. The very journalists and newspapers who falsely vilified the man now adore him and place him on a pedestal.

What is more extraordinary is that the experience never soured Robson or altered his love for – and commitment to – his country. To those who know him well this comes as no surprise, for, as a player, he never sold or gave away his international tickets at Wembley. He attended every England game he could and carried on when he became a manager. He never refused to release club players for international games, even when, in one memorable case, his own club, Ipswich, had an important fixture that clashed. He gave up his skipper Mick Mills because Ron Greenwood was struggling for players.

Since his retirement from the job after the World Cup in Italy in 1990, there have been at least two occasions when he was ready to resume the England mantle in times of deep despair as others failed.

Of course he remembers the bad times, but he prefers to recall the good times – and there were plenty of those. Bobby relished every match in his 95-game international management career. He won 47 of those, drew 29 and lost 19, his team scoring 154 goals and conceding 60. As well as taking England back into the World Cup Finals after two failed attempts before him, Robson produced a great attacking side, often with two wingers. His team only failed to qualify for the first tournament he entered, and they recorded the first ever England away wins in places such as Brazil, the Soviet Union and Yugoslavia.

Most importantly, all his sides had great character. They were never more dangerous than when they were being written off and ridiculed. He introduced individualistic players like John Barnes and Paul Gascoigne and always believed in attack being the best form of defence.

"I had a good team around me. I didn't have any fools. They were well up in the game and their judgement was spot on."

Jimmy Hill and a number of other well-placed, knowledgeable football people publicly told Robson not to go to Brazil and face humiliation in 1984 after a series of results had seen them lose to Wales, draw with Scotland and lose at home to the Soviet Union before a summer tour. Robson's reply to that was to throw in youngsters like teenager John Barnes and Second Division twenty-three-year-old Mark Hateley. England won for the first time ever at the Maracana stadium and by two clear goals.

Robson faced similar problems in the World Cup. In Mexico in 1986, when hooliganism was at its height, making England the most hated nation in the competition, Bobby lost his crucial skipper, Bryan Robson, with a dislocated shoulder, had Ray Wilkins sent off, lost 1–0 to Portugal and only drew 0–0 with Morocco. He and his team were written off, with the vitriol dripping off the pages of the broadsheets as well as the tabloids. The answer was a 3–0 victory over Poland, with a magnificent Lineker hat-trick to qualify, followed by a 3–0

103

thrashing of a violent Paraguay, before Maradona punched England out in the quarter-finals in a 2–1 defeat.

The fact that England went into the World Cup Finals in Italy as one of the favourites is a measure of how much Robson had turned the team round. This was based on a run that had seen them unbeaten since the disastrous European Championship Finals in Germany in 1988, when illness and injury crippled the squad and they lost all three group games to the Republic of Ireland, Holland and Russia.

Surviving the demands once again for his head – he even offered his resignation – Robson, with very much the same squad that had been derided and criticized, launched on a seventeen-game unbeaten run, which only ended in a friendly at Wembley on 22 May 1990 against the talented Uruguayan squad.

This was followed by a 1–1 draw in Tunisia and, when the World Cup began for England in Cagliari on a stormy night in 1990, Robson and his team found themselves under media pressure once more as they drew a horribly scrappy game with the Republic of Ireland 1–1, despite having a host of chances to win it easily.

A goalless draw with Holland and a nervous 1–0 win over Egypt, thanks to a Mark Wright goal from his sweeper position, saw England squeeze through the group stages.

It was a nail-biting time as David Platt scored the extra-time winner against Belgium with penalties looming yet again, then two penalties from Gary Lineker rescued England from a 2–1 defeat against African outsiders Cameroon – England were in the semi-finals with a thrilling 3–2 victory.

West Germany were the next opposition, and the growing confidence and togetherness of the England squad, despite the loss again of skipper Bryan Robson, had Bobby Robson honestly believing they could win not only this game but also the World Cup itself, with a poor Argentina the likely rivals in the final.

Sadly it was not to be, as on another cruel day, England, the better team, battled back from a freak goal from Brehme, deflected over Peter Shilton off Paul

English managerial talent. (Left to right) Robson enjoys a game of golf with Dave Sexton (Chelsea), Alan Ashman (WBA), Bertie Mee (Arsenal) and Don Howe (Arsenal assistant) before the start of the 1970 World Cup in Mexico.

Parker's thigh, and then equalized through the remarkable Gary Lineker in the eightieth minute. With England looking the favourites, the game went into extra time, the third in succession for England, and then into penalties.

Stuart Pearce cruelly saw his kick stopped by the legs of the diving Illgner, and Chris Waddle drove the ball over the crossbar. The dream was over…and so was Bobby Robson's career as England manager.

There was just the unwanted and unneeded third place play-off against Italy, and then it was off to join PSV Eindhoven in Holland. Robson was leaving the job he loved above all others at exactly the moment the public and the newspapers decided what a great England manager he was!

106

"Scouting for Ron Greenwood at the 1982 World Cup in Spain was a great eye-opener."

In charge of the "three lions". Brian Clough (above) was beaten to the position of England manager by Bobby Robson.

Photographed at the 1982 World Cup Finals in Spain (*opposite, top*) Robson (centre) with the man he succeeded as manager, Ron Greenwood (right), and future manager Terry Venables (left). Robson and Venables acted as scouts for Greenwood in England's unbeaten but unsuccessful run in the competition.

Robson (*opposite, bottom*) sits with the man who later replaced him as England manager, Graham Taylor. This was taken in 1982, when Taylor looked after the England Youth team on a part-time basis.

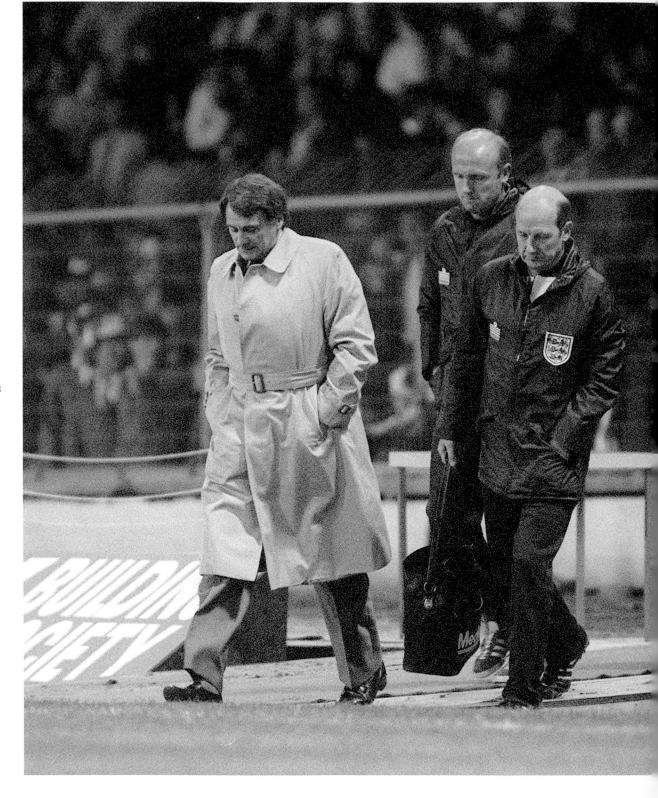

Defeat was not tolerated. England lose a friendly international to West Germany at Wembley, going down 2–1 in a disappointing performance in Robson's first game in charge on 13 October 1982. The anguish shows on the face of Bobby (left) as he walks past the home crowd, followed by a glum-looking Fred Street, the popular England physiotherapist (second from right); Bobby's right-hand man, Don Howe (second from left); and future England manager – if only very briefly – Howard Wilkinson (right). Life was never comfortable when England lost, especially when it was to the old enemy, West Germany, and even more so when it was at Wembley. Robson knew that he would face a battering from the tabloids the next morning, and he subsequently found himself in the middle of a press war between red tops the *Daily Mirror* and the *Sun*.

"In the cynical world of professional football there is a warmth of feeling towards him that is not only remarkable but totally unique."

GARY LINEKER

110   **That winning feeling.** Sometimes the result and the performance lived up to expectations. The warmth of the smiles (from left to right) of England's physiotherapist, Fred Street, assistant physiotherapist, Norman Medhurst, and Bobby Robson tell it all as England canter to a 3–0 victory over Greece, despite the fierce atmosphere in Salonika.

This win was Robson's first as England manager and was welcomed just a month after the German defeat. He was helped in the noisy and expectant Kaftatoglion Stadium by a goal from Tony Woodcock just two minutes into the game. Peter Shilton then kept England in the game before Woodcock scored again, with Sammy Lee, on his debut and in a pair of borrowed boots, finally putting the European Championship tie out of the Greeks' reach.

112

"He wants things done the right way: tuck your shirt in, pull

TERRY BUTCHER

up your socks, and he doesn't like this and doesn't like that."

"Everybody is human, and it does hurt. You try to ignore it and not let it upset you and I think I tried very hard to do that."

Sometimes the manager has little say in where England play. As well as the draws for the European and World Cups, there are friendlies and tours. On this occasion Bobby Robson and his England team inherited a trip to Australia, when all anyone wanted to do was to rest on a beach and forget about football. It was an unhappy tour, with a number of top players missing. England drew 0–0 in Sydney, won 1–0 in Brisbane and then drew 1–1 in Melbourne. Bobby's expression shows exactly what he thinks of the entire enterprise, as he sits head-in-hands beside an equally stern Dave Sexton and Fred Street on the bench.

The ups and downs of England football management.
FA Chairman, the late Bert Millichip (*above, right*), a
favourite of Bobby's, expresses his opinion as England find
they are drawn to play in Monterrey, northern Mexico, in
the 1986 World Cup Finals, with Portugal, Morocco and
Poland as their opponents.

Wherever England play the press will be. Bobby (*right*)
talks with the regulars Steve Curry, Bryon Butler, Bob
Harris (back right) and Bob Driscoll.

Previous pages. Bobby is in glorious isolation in front of
his bench in a World Cup qualifying game against Turkey
in Istanbul. This was the one that the Turkish fans really
fancied, and the crowd filled the stadium hours before
kick-off. They went home disappointed, though, as
England won 8–0.

121

More than football. It's not just the press
Bobby has to contend with (*left*) as England
manager – it is the supporters as well. No
sooner had the 1986 World Cup draw been
made in December 1985 than he was off
to Mexico to sort out hotels and training
facilities. Word had reached ahead and with
memories of the Hysel Stadium disaster fresh
in the Mexicans' minds, he was greeted with
headlines in *El Sol* (*The Sun*) of "THE
ANIMALS ARE COMING!".

England were in Mexico for a pre-World
Cup tournament when the Liverpool fans ran
riot in the European Cup Final against
Juventus in Belgium. Bobby (*above*) talks with
his skipper Bryan Robson before the dramatic
friendly against Italy a few days later.

"I used to like joining in with the training but I don't do that now because I'm not good enough any more."

Bobby training with his players. Robson shows the effort (*opposite*) in June 1985 in Los Angeles before a friendly against the USA, with full back Kenny Sansom offering a helping hand. By 1986 (*above*) he seems to have learnt his lesson, as he takes an easier option during an England training session in Monterrey, Mexico, where the high altitude made life even more difficult. Robson always has been, and still is, a tracksuit manager. If he hangs up that tracksuit it will be on his way out of the game.

Overleaf. A happy Bobby Robson before the controversial game against Argentina in Mexico City, when a tear would eventually replace the smile.

"I was quite composed about it for two or three seconds because I thought he was obviously going to give us a free kick. Then I saw the linesman running up and I turned to Don and said 'I think he has given it.'"

A critical moment. This is when all the careful preparation put into the Mexico World Cup by Bobby Robson and his technical team were undone by the left hand of Argentinian Diego Maradona, an unsighted Tunisian referee and his inexperienced linesman. The handball "goal" was allowed to stand and Maradona went on to score another four minutes later, this time a legitimate and spectacular solo goal. England fought back bravely with Gary Lineker scoring a goal and narrowly missing another. On the final whistle Robson's dreams of a World Cup Final disappeared amid tears and anger.

"Despite the problems he still talked to the press on a daily basis. He still gave them too much."

TERRY BUTCHER

128   **England press conferences were held in some strange places.**
This one was in a Dusseldorf dug-out before a friendly against West Germany in September 1987. Robson announced that Peter Shilton would skipper the side the next day, with Viv Anderson, Kenny Sansom, Glenn Hoddle, Tony Adams, Gary Mabbutt, Peter Reid, John Barnes, Peter Beardsley, Gary Lineker and Chris Waddle. The assembled British press, including Steve Curry, Bob Driscoll, Jeff Powell, David Meek, Brian Woolnough and Paddy Barclay, don't look convinced by the team. Lineker went on to score but England still lost 3–1.

Looking to the heavens. Bobby (*opposite*) reflects in Riyadh after a disappointing 1–1 draw with Saudi Arabia in a friendly on 16 November 1988. Earlier in the year, England had drawn 0–0 with Israel in Tel Aviv. This was yet another poor result that had the football writers sharpening their pencils, while his old team-mate Jimmy Hill (*above, right*) was as forthright as ever about his friend on BBC television. Despite the ongoing war of words with both press and television, Bobby retained his dignity and his temper throughout.

"[Don] was very sensible, very intelligent and he was very supportive of me. He stood with me."

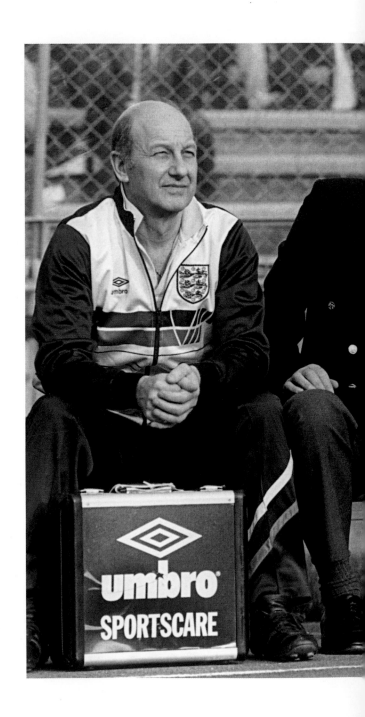

132   **No such thing as a friendly.** Another drawn game, this one 0–0 with Hungary in Budapest, in a friendly in April 1988. The famous Nep Stadium in Budapest offered Bobby about as much comfort as the result, as he and his right-hand man Don Howe discuss the team's problems. Bobby knew that there was no such thing as a "friendly" back home, and it was expected that he win games regardless of the development of the team or experimentation. Even away draws like this one were dissected and abused by the critics and supporters alike, as victory was demanded in every game. Bobby, however, remained level-tempered, even with the sternest of his critics, and rarely refused to answer a question at a press conference.

134

"We talked about the quality of his coaching and how he is able to coach a team... he explains in a gentle way not in an aggressive way."

FRANZ BECKENBAUER

Sometimes a draw away from home was good. Bobby (*above*) can't contain his glee in his post-match press conference when England came through a tough World Cup qualifying test against Poland in Chorzow in the build-up to the 1990 World Cup Finals with a point from a goalless draw.

While he looked happy behind the microphone on this occasion (*above*), he was never happier than when he was wearing his tracksuit holding a ball under his arm (*opposite*). Here he is coaching the England team at their superb training facilities at Bisham Abbey in Buckinghamshire in September 1988, shortly before their 1–0 home win against Denmark. Neil Webb scored the only goal of the game at Wembley.

Memories of the Rous Cup. Sir Stanley Rous, the great English administrator, may not have approved of this friendly end-of-season competition named after him. This was the 1988 tournament, with Don Howe (left) sitting quietly while Bobby gets excited during the 1–1 draw with Colombia at Wembley. The goal, almost inevitably, came from Gary Lineker. England beat Scotland and Switzerland to win the trophy, which was held five times by England during the 1980s. It did England little good, however, as they had a disastrous European Championship afterwards, losing in Germany to Ireland, Holland and Russia.

137

"That is why Don has been a close associate of mine and why I have loved the fella, and I mean love him. He has been a great, great guy for me, Don has. We played together and finished together."

The best of friends, the closest of colleagues. 139

The bond between Bobby and Don Howe was formed at West Bromwich Albion and has continued unabated ever since. The two interacted together perfectly, especially during their eight years with England. Don always accepted his role as assistant, and did not push his own opinion unless asked – even then, he knew that his old team-mate would think about it and make up his own mind. The two were such a good pair that often they would be thinking along the same lines. Here they can be seen in tandem at Bisham Abbey on a wet day in April 1989, two days before their 5–0 World Cup qualifying victory against Albania at Wembley.

"When he talked you listened and you walk away feeling very positive as well as getting a bollocking."

PAUL GASCOIGNE

Two Geordies together (*opposite*). Bobby Robson and Paul Gascoigne pictured together during training. What a pity it was that Gazza never played for Bobby at club level, because the manager seemed to have the magic touch with the player he described as "daft as a brush". Having turned him down as a teenager at Ipswich, Robson turned the wayward wonder boy into a world star in the 1990 World Cup Finals in Italy.

Bobby (*above*) appears to be praying for divine intervention in Stockholm in 1989, the day before a goalless draw against Sweden in a World Cup qualifying match.

"You feel like you are going to go through a brick wall for him. You want to do things beyond the normal for Bobby Robson."

Loyalty and respect. A bloody Terry Butcher, after a clash with Ekstrom, leaves the pitch following a stunning display in England's goalless draw in a vital World Cup qualifying game against Sweden in Stockholm in 1989. Butcher was Robson's rock, not only during the glory years at Ipswich, but also for much of his eight-year reign with England. Butcher was, without doubt, a Robson man, a real man. He was big, strong, muscular, reliable, a good leader, a fierce competitor and totally loyal to the man he held in the greatest respect. That feeling was completely mutual. Butcher pulled on the England shirt seventy-seven times for England during his long and distinguished career with Ipswich and Glasgow Rangers, and never once gave less than one hundred per cent both as an individual and a team man. As captain he was a fearsome warrior who would score points off the opposition by growling or shouting at them in the tunnel before the game, but off the pitch he was a charming, friendly and intelligent, gentle giant.

*"I never forget the World Cup Finals
in Italy. We were a whisker away.
I felt if we got through we would
have actually beaten Argentina."*

Emotions at the opposite ends of the spectrum. David Platt (*opposite*) wheels away to celebrate the late extra-time winner in the 2–1 victory over Belgium in Bologna in June 1990. He spectacularly converted Paul Gascoigne's clever free kick in the dying minutes with a penalty shoot-out looming. The German captain Lothar Matthaeus (*below*) generously consoles Chris Waddle after the England winger missed a penalty in the shoot-out against West Germany in the semi-final in Turin. England had more than held their own and looked set for their first World Cup Final for almost a quarter of a century, only for Waddle to shoot over the crossbar and Stuart Pearce to hit the goalkeeper's legs.

Overleaf. Bobby Robson consoles Chris Waddle, Paul Gascoigne and Gary Lineker as he tries to hide his personal devastation after losing on penalties to Germany.

"It was much better me leaving after 1990 than in 1988."

The two faces of Bobby Robson. On the left, the suntanned, smiling Robson, ready for the challenge of the England job that he had dreamed about. While above, the hair is grey, the smile is a flicker in a field of desolation, the facial lines are more pronounced and the eyes are sad. This is what eight years of managing England did to him. Yet despite the trials and tribulations, the battles with the newspapers and the more secretive conflicts with certain members of the International Committee, he let it be known that he was ready to return to the hottest seat in football at the drop of a hat. It was not so much a job for Bobby Robson as a calling.

8   An Englishman Abroad

Although Bobby Robson left his England job a hero, there remained a bitter taste in the mouth when, before travelling to the World Cup Finals in Italy, he was accused of being a traitor to his country by accepting a managerial role with PSV Eindhoven before the World Cup Finals began.

Robson had accepted the job because FA Chief Executive Graham Kelly had informed him that they would not be offering him a new contract after the World Cup and that he was free to find alternative employment. Having confirmed with the chairman Bert Millichip that not even winning the World Cup itself – something he was desperately close to doing - would change the situation, he finally agreed to a two-year contract with PSV, a side who had been chasing him for over a year.

"It was a more-than-happy two-year stay in Holland. I loved the players..."

Robson was a great admirer of the Dutch game, having signed Thijssen and Muhren, played against the top Dutch clubs in Europe and faced the national side several times as England manager. He would have preferred to stay with England but this was a good second choice.

For a start, PSV was handy, had an excellent stadium, were backed by the giant electrical company Philips, and were desperate to win back their Dutch title. Robson returned home for one day after the World Cup Finals in Italy, then caught the ferry from Harwich to the Hook of Holland and started his new job the next morning at 10 am.

Robson enjoyed a happy two-year stay in Holland with people who were pro-English, a club with dignity and style and a press who were not nearly as intrusive or abusive as the English newspapers. In fact, Robson took more criticism from the English papers when PSV went out of Europe and the Dutch Cup early on than he did from the Dutch press.

The first season was a struggle, not least because of the loss of his main striker, Romario, who was out from September to January with an injury. Romario was

Older and wiser.
Bobby Robson begins his European adventure in Holland.

151

sorely missed, and it was not until the final day of the 1990–91 season that Robson saw his team capture the Dutch title, while thinking how in the past he had lost the English Championship on the last day of the season.

Challengers and defending champions Ajax were playing Vitesse at home, while Bobby's team met Volendam in the Philips Stadium, holding a two-goal advantage. Ajax were quickly a goal up, but PSV matched them almost shot for shot as both scored three times without reply.

Robson's two seasons in Holland were separated by a close season tour to India, a real eye-opener for Robson as he witnessed the vast crowds, including one of 100,000 people at Salt Lake Stadium.

The second season was another triumph as Robson guided PSV to a back-to-back Championship, beating Feyenoord first and then the inevitable Ajax, finishing three points clear with only one defeat and dropping only ten points all season.

The big frustration for Robson was the team's failure in Europe. After putting out Besiktas of Turkey in the first round, they were defeated by Anderlecht, which Robson was disappointed about but not surprised by, as he was missing five of his star players, including, again, Romario.

The two years were both productive and educational for Robson. The two Dutch Championships looked good on his CV and, for the first time, he worked with a general manager, Kees Ploegsma, who took from Robson the burden of arranging travel, negotiating contracts and organizing transfers. Robson would offer a shortlist of the players he felt were needed and Ploegsma and his staff would set about trying to arrange them. Robson's duties were to organize training, pick the team and the tactics and win the trophies.

It was assumed when Bobby left after two years that he had been dismissed because of the club's failure in Europe, but it was simply that he had reached the end of his two-year contract and PSV wanted someone else. Hans Westerhof, the Groningen coach, was his sucessor, but he still failed in Europe and lost the Dutch title into the bargain the following season.

There were, however, no regrets from Robson, because he had enjoyed the experience of his two years in Holland, of the different style of football and the different approach to management. He still carried the baggage of England with him and withstood considerable sniping, including the accusation that he had been relieved of his authority for the final match of the first season when, in truth, he had invited his assistant Hans Dorjee to take the final training session as a gesture before he left to take his new job as manager of Feyenoord. After eight years as manager of England that sort of spin from the English press was relatively easy to handle.

"... I made many new friends amongst the lovely Dutch people. That is why I eventually went back there."

In the second season, Robson had promoted Frank Arnesen to the role of assistant and found in him not only an excellent coach but also a good friend. The two travelled to games together and became very close.

Robson also made friendships, although of a different nature, with some of the players. Stan Valckx, the big central defender, would run through brick walls for his coach, while Eric Gerets, the Belgian international, was a strong captain who went on to become a top coach in his home country before taking over from Robson after his second spell at PSV.

Robson was also grateful to have a decent goalkeeper in Hans van Breukelen, who signed a new two-year contract when the newspapers predicted he was going to walk out on the club, and Barry van Aerle, who provided the light relief in the dressing room.

Robson would undoubtedly have done even better had he had a fully fit Romario. Although, even when fit, this outstanding Brazilian went out dancing and clubbing before games, kept popping home to Brazil and refused to travel with the team to India, he was their star player. Romario did not always pull his weight on the pitch but, invariably, he was the match winner and Robson, for once not in charge of his players' off-field behaviour, was happy to put up with his idiosyncrasies.

153

Leading by example.
Bobby on his first day
at PSV in July 1990.

The other difference Robson discovered after his years in England was the lack of depth in the Dutch League; in those days, PSV competed with Ajax and Feyenoord for all the trophies. In fact, in that second and last season in Eindhoven, while Bobby won the title, Feyenoord took the Cup and Ajax the UEFA Cup.

Bobby left Holland with many more friends than enemies. Such was his popularity that, at the end of the 1998 season, when he finally left Barcelona, he was hijacked and returned to do another year with PSV while they waited for his old captain, Gerets, to complete his contractual obligations in Belgium.

This time, Bobby filled the void left by the departing Dick Advocaat, and his job was to steady the ship and, if possible, earn a place in the Champions League for Gerets the next season, when new players would be brought in. As it transpired, PSV beat Ajax to win the Dutch Super Cup and finished third to clinch a place in the lucrative Champions League.

It was a satisfying return, as, before he arrived, Robson lost a number of players to other clubs: Boudewijn Zenden and Philip Cocu, ironically, to Barcelona, Jaap Stam to Manchester United, Wim Jonk to Sheffield Wednesday and Arthur Numan, following Advocaat, to Glasgow Rangers. Worse was to come with the loss of Ernest Faber, Stan Valckx, Ovidiu Stinga, Luc Nilis and others to long-term injuries.

The one big bonus to Robson in this difficult season was the goal-scoring skills of the then winger Ruud van Nistelrooy, a player Robson was eventually to recommend to Sir Alex Ferguson at Manchester United.

The final game of the season was against Alkmaar at the Philips Stadium and Robson asked his players to see him off in style. They so did with a 7–0 win and the manager was paraded around the pitch on a lap of honour to a standing ovation from the spectators. A deserved accolade from a crowd who knew the incredible problems their caretaker boss had overcome that season.

It was a poignant moment for Bobby Robson, as he had no idea of what lay

in front of him now he had decided to return home to England. PSV had provided an interesting diversion en route from Barcelona but it had also convinced him he still had something to offer the game. His enthusiasm was undimmed and his knowledge had grown year by year. He was fired up for another last tilt at English football...but where?

> **"I have been very lucky and worked with some very good players."**

A new life, a new beginning. PSV Eindhoven, despite the backing of electrical giants Philips, had failed to live up to expectations until the arrival of Bobby Robson, fresh from the World Cup semi-finals in Italy. Robson delivered two domestic titles, resisting the Ajax and Feyenoord clubs, and gave them players like the brilliant young striker Ronaldo (*opposite*), but it was not enough. When his contract expired they were happy to say thank you and let him move on, because he had failed to make an impact in Europe.

Robson brought with him to Eindhoven his great passion for the game, as he shows (*above*), watched by a surprised General Manager Kees Ploegsma (second left) and his assistant trainer Hans Dorjee (left) in an August pre-season friendly against Belgian side KV Mechelen.

"He made every player in the team better than they really were. I never met a person who was so passionate about something."

RUUD VAN NISTELROOY

On the brink. Both Bobby and his assistant Hans Dorjee (above) know just what it will take to win the Dutch title from Ajax – a minimum of a two-goal margin. This was the target in the final game of the 1990–91 season as they faced FC Volendam on 16 June 1991 in Eindhoven. The objective was achieved as PSV won 3–0 to clinch the Dutch crown.

One of the young players Robson brought through was striker Ruud van Nistelrooy (*opposite*), who has since regularly paid tribute to his English manager for bringing him on and then recommending him to Sir Alex Ferguson at Manchester United.

"My biggest disappointment in Holland was our failure to make an impression in Europe despite winning the title two years on the trot."

Excess baggage. Robson's first two years at PSV Eindhoven were, in many ways, transitional, as he tried to shrug off the aftermath of his eight years as England manager. His every move and, in particular, every defeat, were watched and reported on back in England as his detractors willed him to fail in his first job abroad. The fact that he was able to reshape the team and lead them to two successive Dutch titles when they weren't favourites speaks volumes not only about his management skills in football but also his ability to remain calm in the face of severe provocation. He rarely blew his top, despite some steamy press conferences, and he is always welcomed back at every club he has served.

9   Bobby Five O

Bobby Robson had made up his mind at the end of his two-year stint at PSV that he would return home to England, but when Sporting Lisbon stepped in towards the end of the second season, the prospect of a couple of years in the sun in Portugal was too strong a pull.

He would, he thought, do his two years and then retire – after all, he surmised, he would be sixty and who would want him then?

What really decided it for him was that Sporting presented a completely different challenge in a new setting plus a considerable hike in salary. Such was his relationship with PSV that they were made fully aware of the situation and even allowed him to make several trips to Portugal to finalize the details.

"He taught me to see that life is not just the good things and sometimes you pass bad moments and you learn with that to improve and get more strong."

LUIS FIGO

It did not frighten Bobby that it was a new language in a new country with a new style of football. What did concern him, however, was the media interest. Before he left home, a flock of Portuguese journalists besieged his house in Ipswich, while on arrival at Lisbon he found another group waiting for him, along with a huge number of fans plus Sporting's president Sousa Cintra and a young assistant, José Mourinho, who was to follow him to Porto and Barcelona as Robson's career moved on.

163

Robson appointed the former Sporting player Manuel Fernandes as coach and set about looking at the players he had on offer, before going back to Holland to buy Stan Valckx and the Ukrainian Sergei Cherbakov to add to stars like Luis Figo, Jorge Cadete and Krasimir Balakov.

Happy to be home.
A relaxed Bobby prepares Sporting Lisbon for a friendly against his beloved Newcastle in 1992.

The club had won nothing for more than ten years when he arrived and clearly there was a great deal of work to be done to turn around its fortunes. With the aid of a few more signings, Robson lifted Sporting to third place in the Portuguese league behind Porto and Benfica, but there was enough of an improvement for Robson to hold great hope for the next season, especially when the president brought in Antonio

Pacheco and Paulo Sousa from Benfica. Robson had nothing to do with the signings and thanked his lucky stars they were players he rated, avoiding a conflict with the president, who had an inflated view of his knowledge of the game.

The players had responded to Robson and, with an average team age of twenty-three, he fancied a serious go at the title as they went straight to the top of the table and beat Celtic in the UEFA Cup.

Early in December, Sporting beat Salzburg 2–0 in the UEFA Cup. They should have won by more, but they still looked comfortable to progress further. However, there was a blow before the second leg when Robson was forced to bring in reserve goalkeeper Paulo Costinha, another of Cintra's personal buys. Costinha promptly let in a goal from thirty-five yards out; with time running out another one flew in from long distance and in extra time Paulo conceded a third one from a corner.

On the flight home the president berated the players over the intercom and two days later he dismissed his English manager, the first time Robson had been sacked in twenty-five years. The reason for this ridiculous decision quickly became obvious when Cintra appointed Carlos Querois, who had just quit the Portuguese national team, a personal friend of the president and an academic who had never played the game professionally.

A week earlier Robson had once again turned down Everton, while Wales came in for him a little later, but unfortunately the salary on offer was disappointing.

The players were as upset as Robson. They threw him a party and made a presentation to him, only for the evening to be shattered when Cherbakov crashed his car after the party. The club immediately stopped the young Ukrainian's salary and it was only the generosity of Robson and the other players that kept him afloat. He was never to play again.

Robson then planned to travel to the Caribbean to fulfil a long-held dream of watching England play cricket against the West Indies, but the trip was hastily cancelled when Porto president Pinto da Costa offered him the management of FC Porto, a large club who had been underachieving. They promised him a huge

"There was a wicked touch of revenge about managing Porto so soon after losing my job at Sporting, and I knew from my own experience they were a side full of good players."

pay rise and a two-and-a-half-year contract. Having already had his fingers burnt, he asked for just eighteen months, and signed a contract after a day's thought on 31 January 1994, starting immediately.

Porto were in a slump and their negative play had driven away the fans. Robson immediately changed the system, got rid of the sweeper and in a short time became known as "Bobby Five O", because his team kept winning 5–0!

The team took off but nothing is ordinary in Portugal and Robson suddenly found himself taking training in the club car park as the ground had been shut down because of an unpaid tax bill.

Undaunted, Robson carried on the chase of Benfica and Porto finished closely in second place – and ahead of Sporting who had been top when Robson left. To cap a self-satisfying season, Porto beat Sporting 2–1 to win the Portuguese Cup.

The next time Robson returned to the Sporting Lisbon stadium was the night on which Porto won the League title, and to make a perfect evening even more memorable he was tossed in the air by his delighted players and applauded all round the pitch by the home supporters, who remembered him with great affection.

Robson, in his one-and-a-half seasons, had transformed the team and the results, bringing in a host of new players. It was all going so well, until tragedy struck again, when another youngster, Rui Filipe, was killed in a car crash. In that tragic accident and the one that ended the career of the young Ukrainian neither player was wearing a seat belt.

Soon afterwards, with Porto top of the table and close to sell-out crowds every week, Robson was offered – and accepted – a new, improved deal, adding one verbal proviso that if a major club came in for him he would be allowed to go. That was immediately put to the test in May 1995, when Arsenal asked him to take the seat vacated by George Graham at Highbury – a job Robson had long coveted. He was thrilled at the prospect and was ready to fly to Switzerland the next day to inform Pinto da Costa. But the president claimed he could not remember the agreement and refused to give his permission, despite the fact that the conversation had been witnessed by José Mourinho.

Following the game.
Bobby looks out onto
the pitch towards his
Sporting Lisbon side.

Robson and Arsenal offered compensation, but Da Costa said no and Robson was reluctant to break a contract, as it was something he had never done in his life, while Arsenal were also unhappy to take that path in view of their recent problems with their previous manager.

Da Costa showed his other side a few months later when Robson was diagnosed with life-threatening cancer and he kept Robson's position open for as long as he needed. Robson, typically, came back long before his surgeon's recommendation and Porto finished the season top of the table, thirteen points ahead of Sporting and seventeen in front of Benfica.

With two titles and having worked the extra year, Robson felt all duties to Da Costa had been honourably discharged and when Barcelona came knocking for the third time in his career Robson accepted their contract and told Da Costa there was no turning back. Da Costa accepted, but ungraciously withheld wages and bonuses to the value of a quarter of a million pounds.

Robson began to wonder about the Portuguese system, for he had been left with tax debts that Sporting were supposed to have paid according to his contract. In fact, worse was to follow, as a year later he received yet another Inland Revenue bill for over £100,000, leading to court cases.

For all the problems Robson had encountered, he enjoyed his four years in Portugal and clearly Portugal liked him, for when problems arose at Barcelona a year or so later both Sporting and their bigger Lisbon neighbours, Benfica, were jostling for his services. Bobby was tempted because he loved the country, the people and the sense of history in managing the country's three top clubs, something no one else had ever done previously. It was the second time Benfica had approached Robson in a matter of months.

It may sound strange that Sporting came back after sacking him and not paying what was due, but the hierarchy had changed and they were keen to make amends, even though the salary was scarcely an incentive to take him away from the exciting challenge of Barcelona.

Europe was now Bobby's playground. He looks relaxed and comfortable in Italy (*above and opposite*) in March 1995 as Porto visit the Italian side Sampdoria. After his experiences with Ipswich Town winning the European Cup Winners' Cup, he was always happy in European competition, relishing the challenge, the change in style and the different tactical approaches from unknown players. The people loved his passion for the game and they always made him feel welcome. He turned around an ailing side, packed the stadium, and filled the trophy cabinet with League and Cup trophies. He left the club with mixed feelings about President Pinto da Costa (*above, left*), who refused to allow him to move to Arsenal, but who stood by him when he had to undergo surgery for life-threatening cancer.

Overleaf. Bobby Robson takes his Porto side to the Nou Camp to face his future club Barcelona in the semi-finals of the UEFA Champions League in April 1994.

170

1 0   The Buffer Zone

Bobby Robson and Barcelona were clearly destined for each other. Three times the Catalan giants came for the services of the English manager, and only finally landed him at the third attempt in 1996.

It was the opportunity Robson had always dreamed about, he called it his destiny, but what he didn't know was that the club and their president, Josep Lluis Nunez, and Robson's long-term friend Joan Gaspart, were using him as a buffer between the bitter, sacked Johan Cruyff and the appointment of another Dutchman, Louis van Gaal.

It was the small print in the document that caught Robson out. It stipulated that in the second year of the contract they could move him from coach to manager. He raised an eyebrow and asked a question or two but considered that if he had a good season they were hardly likely to take such action.

173

Robson quickly forgot about the in-fighting as he surveyed his new home, the 120,000-seat Nou Camp Stadium, its reserve pitch next door with accommodation for another 25,000 and his squad of players. He was in his element, except for the shadow of Cruyff hanging over him and the club. The Dutchman had been incredibly successful and popular both as a player and as a coach, but two years without a trophy was too long for Nunez as he looked anxiously towards his re-election.

The situation served to throw Robson under the microscope, with half of the city ready to criticize him for whatever happened, while the other half demanded instant success. Even the best start for thirty-three years did not deflect this and Robson could not understand why the criticism continued to flow, despite having a winning side scoring goals and playing exciting football. He admitted to me, "As a coach I could do no right!"

Imagine winning 6–0 at home in front of 85,000 fans and being slammed by the press the next day for not playing football. That happened in January 1997

> *"I was working with him in Portugal and I found him again in Barcelona ... that time was a difficult year for him."*
>
> Luis Figo

Third time of asking.
After Bobby finally arrived at the Nou Camp he discovered there was a secret agenda.

when they beat Rayo Vallecano, and again when they staged the most stunning comeback of the decade – beating Atlético Madrid 5–4 after being three down – thanks to Robson's innovative and dramatic substitutions. The press, ludicrously, put that one down to player power.

Robson, throughout, retained his dignity and did not criticize anyone, especially Cruyff, who sat at the back of the stand for every game, hurting Bobby with his presence but being fully justified as he watched not only his team but also his son Jordi play. There was simply nothing Robson could say or do – other than keep on winning. He also partly solved the problem when he sold Jordi to Manchester United, saving the aggravation that would have surely followed if he had left out the son of the popular former manager.

Robson wondered what he could do to satisfy his detractors. He had taken the team straight to the top of the league, they were scoring for fun and, the cherry on the cake, he had given them the Brazilian Ronaldo, their new super-hero, pushing through the deal despite doubts from the board over the fee.

"I have learned how to handle them individually. I have learned about man management."

Robson's experience with the English press gave him only a slight indication of what lay in wait for him in Barcelona, with journalists having to fill many column inches and daily radio and television programmes about the team.

He continued to take fearful flak, despite losing only eight games all season. Barcelona went on to win the European Cup Winners' Cup, the Spanish Cup and the Spanish Super Cup. They finished second in La Liga, the Spanish league, two points behind Real Madrid, who, that season, played fourteen games less than their great rivals. Any other team and it would not have mattered nearly as much.

Robson also lost Giovanni and Ronaldo for seven or eight games apiece when they were required for Brazil. In fact, every player was an international on call for their respective countries, and the schedule was too heavy to have games called off.

"I didn't know they were going to bring van Gaal in. I didn't know."

Three trophies and second place was clearly not enough, and Robson began to think that something was happening when Louis van Gaal appeared on Dutch television early in 1997 and hinted about what was to happen.

Gradually, realization dawned on him, as did the reason for that strange clause in his contract, and another which stated he would have to pay the club double what he was paid if he walked out, some two million pounds. But still he believed if his team kept winning they could not move him upstairs.

Bobby did what he does best. After a bad February, when his worst fears were being confirmed, he rolled up his sleeves, got his team playing and lost only two of the remaining twenty-five games. But those two games proved to be crucial. Barça lost 3–1 to Valladolid after leading 1–0, and on the same day Real came back from 0–2 to beat Bilbao 4–2. Had the games gone the other way, Barcelona would have won La Liga at a canter.

But what really crucified Robson and his team was the last-day defeat to bottom-of-the-table Hercules, which meant their great rivals finished two points clear, despite having won one game fewer and scored seventeen goals fewer over the season. However, Robson still managed to finish the season in a blaze of glory as they came back from behind to beat Real Betis with a Figo winner six minutes from time in the Bernabeu. They also won the European Cup Winners' Cup 1–0 against Paris Saint-Germain at the De Kuip Stadium in Rotterdam, thanks to a Ronaldo penalty. Even his detractors had to admit that the manager had done remarkably well and that Bobby had never lost faith in his own ability.

It was not until June that Robson's now obvious departure from his post was confirmed, or, indeed, his replacement by van Gaal, who was to become the highest paid manager in the world.

Bobby was, however, distraught that he would not be able to challenge for the European Cup or the European Super Cup, but he was determined to retain his considerable dignity and do the job he was asked to do: scouting the world for talent to keep Barcelona where he had put them – back on top!

There was no question of moving and, indeed, Robson had rejected the one remaining job he really wanted, to manage Newcastle United, when he was approached during his first season of turmoil at Barcelona. Newcastle offered him a five-year contract with a two-year option and a salary to match his money in Spain. Robson sounded out Nunez and Gaspart but was told he could not leave. Everton also came knocking (twenty years after their first approach), as did Celtic, Besiktas, Sporting Lisbon and Benfica. It was a wonderful morale -booster to feel so wanted when he thought he had come to the end of his active career.

Strangely, despite all the problems, Robson never regretted his two years at Barcelona, not even the second year, when, although he didn't hold his cherished position of coach, he became a travelling ambassador and watched football all over the globe.

It was while on his travels in Belgrade, watching Red Star play Partizan, that he bumped into his old friend from PSV, Frank Arnesen, who explained to him the problems they were going to have with Advocaat going to Rangers and Club Brugge refusing to release Gerets from his contract for a further year. Robson was stunned at the salary and bonuses being offered for just one season and eventually agreed to join them when his contract finished with Barcelona. Such were Robson's priorities and own high standards that he refused to look at players for PSV while still doing the same job for Barcelona.

Clearly, Barcelona liked what their Technical Director was doing and, to his surprise, they asked him to stay on while his old club Ipswich and several others tried to tempt him back. But he had given his word to PSV and he was always a man of his word.

During that final year in the Catalan capital Robson had the satisfaction of seeing his team win the "double" and when he eventually left the Nou Camp he was a more popular person than when he first arrived.

Among the scrum.
Bobby Robson is surrounded by television cameras and pressmen on his arrival at Barcelona.

"They used me as a bridge but did not tell me. If they had told me I would not have gone there. They did not think I would do well."

178

Intense media pressure. Bobby thought he had experienced it all until he moved to Barcelona, where even he was stunned by the intensity of the media coverage, the daily press conferences and the thousands of words churned out about the club every day. It was never more intense than when they played their greatest rivals Real Madrid, as Terry Venables was to find out when Bobby suggested the Catalan club should appoint the up-and-coming young Englishman. Venables is pictured (*opposite, right*) with Barça vice president (eventually president) Joan Gaspart in October 1986 after a more than creditable 1–1 draw with their arch-rivals at the Bernabeu Stadium in Madrid.

Bobby (*above*) settles himself into his new job in a pre-season tournament in Barcelona on 21 August 1996, when his new team beat Inter Milan 2–1 in the Olympic Stadium to win the summer title.

"Bobby Robson is an institution who performed wonders while he was in Spain."

Raul

180   **Not quite enough.** Although Robson won three cups during his year in charge at Barcelona, his disappointment was in losing a desperately tight title race to bitter rivals Real Madrid. This is one of the reasons why Bobby (*right*) tries to get his players to give a little more in January 1997 against struggling Hercules in the Nou Camp Stadium, Barcelona. Hercules stunned the Catalan club by upsetting the odds and winning the game 3–2 in one of only a few League defeats for Barça. This cost the English manager a clean sweep of the Spanish trophies and heaped further embarrassment on the Barcelona board, who had already committed themselves to hiring Dutch coach Louis van Gaal.

182

"Then, of course, they were embarrassed and they didn't know what to do with me."

Predicting victory. One of Robson's greatest triumphs was to steer Barcelona to the European Cup Winners' Cup. He predicted a two-goal margin (*above*) against Red Star Belgrade in the second round. Barça won the first leg 3–1, with goals from Giovanni and Figo, in front of 73,000 at the Nou Camp, and then held Red Star Belgrade 1–1 with another goal from Giovanni. Barça had already beaten AEK Larnaca with two Ronaldo goals in the first round and after knocking out Red Star they went on to oust AIK Stockholm 4–2 on aggregate. They then sensationally came back after a 1–1 draw at home against Fiorentina to win 2–0 in Italy and reached the final against Paris St Germain, which Barcelona went on to win.

The conductor (*opposite*) orchestrates a famous victory over Real Madrid on 10 May 1997, with the only goal being scored by his greatest Barcelona signing, Ronaldo.

"To play for Barcelona at 20 isn't easy. Winning and scoring goals bring their own pressures and Bobby Robson showed me how to deal with all of this in my career."

RONALDO

This is it - the one that counts. The brilliant Brazilian Ronaldo (*above*) slots home the penalty that gave Barça their 1–0 European Cup Winners' Cup Final victory over French side Paris St Germain in Rotterdam on 14 May 1997 in front of a sell-out crowd of 45,000. Ronaldo's goal in the thirty-eighth minute was enough to win the trophy, proudly held by the manager (*opposite*), for this was one of his finest victories.

Previous pages. Bobby studiously ignores the drum-beating Atlético Madrid supporter before their game in Madrid on 13 April 1997. In the end it was Bobby beating the drum for Barcelona, as Ronaldo bagged a hat trick in a 5–2 victory.

"And the chairman to be fair to him, he's a nice man, said look 'we would like you to stay'. I said 'what as?', and he replied 'something similar'. I was the best-paid scout in the world, I'm telling you. There was no scout like me... they paid me my trainer's salary."

188

Used as a buffer. For many weeks Bobby Robson refused to believe that Barcelona would appoint Louis van Gaal, the Ajax coach, while he still had a year left of his contract, had won three trophies and gained second place in the Spanish League. He was wrong and had to swallow his pride and take a role as the world's highest-paid scout as Barcelona continued to pay him his agreed salary. Bobby refused to be put down by a decision that had been taken even before he started his job, and, instead of sulking, threw himself into his new task with the same energy that he had put into management. He bore the Dutchman no ill will, as shown when the two went for dinner in a Barcelona restaurant on 30 June 1997 (*opposite*). Bobby Robson, as ever, had acted with great dignity in a situation that would have had many of his fellow managers looking for a quiet, dark room.

11   The Homecoming

When Bobby Robson returned from Holland it was with mixed feelings. He was home at last, but for the first time since losing his first managerial job at Fulham he found himself out of work.

At the age at which most people would retire, and with enough in the bank to follow his ambitions of watching international cricket around the world, he should have been happy walking into the sunset. But he wasn't.

I travelled with him to the Caribbean, where I introduced him in Antigua to one of his heroes, Sir Viv Richards. The feeling was mutual, and he worked with some young coaches and players in St Lucia. The weather was beautiful, the rum splendid and the company was fine – but he could not settle. The football season was about to kick off at home and he was without a job. To make it worse, one club had told him he was too old when he let it be known he was interested in filling their vacancy.

It didn't help when he saw his beloved Newcastle United stumble in their start to the new season under Dutch coach Ruud Gullit. Newcastle, in fact, slipped to second from bottom in the Premiership with only Sheffield Wednesday below them, and suddenly Gullit was out.

Newcastle's entire board, with the exception of Freddy Shepherd, had tried to persuade Robson to return to his native North East while he was at Barcelona, and this time Sir John Hall was not going to mess around. He instructed his senior board members to secure the signature of the man he had been chasing for two years. There was no other name in the minds of the majority.

Robson did not need persuading; indeed, he would have walked back to his home club from his house in Ipswich, and why not, when he always admitted he "bled black and white" from childhood.

His first game in charge, without any time to prepare, was at Chelsea. If he had any doubts about his return to English football after his self-imposed exile,

"You know I was born and bred here. I left in 1950 and came back in 1999 so I was away for almost 50 years."

191

Home at last!
Bobby on his return to St James' Park.

they were swept away in the moments before that game as the entire crowd at Stamford Bridge rose to salute him, Newcastle and Chelsea supporters alike. Was there a hint of a tear in the Robson eye?

Bobby Robson was back, and at the club he most wanted to be a part of. He was welcomed by players, crowds and managers all over the country. Even the press laid out the red carpet. But they were waiting. Everyone was waiting to see whether Robson still had the indefinable "it". Could he turn the club around? His answer was to don his tracksuit and get out there amongst them, coaxing and cajoling in his inimitable style.

Players such as Robert Lee and Alan Shearer, who had been cast aside by the profligate Gullit, were hastened back, and some of the foreign players, who had come, it seemed, simply for the money, found themselves taking a back seat while clubs were found for them.

It did not take long for Alan Shearer to signal his return to the front line by scoring five of an eight-goal thrashing of hapless Sheffield Wednesday. Bobby Robson was back, and with style. But it was no easy ride. Things had to be changed, wages saved, a new stand built, players brought in without breaking the bank and, most important of all, the club secured from the dark threat of relegation.

There was never a doubt. The restored Shearer scored twenty-three goals in the League and five more in cup matches, and the team finished in a very creditable eleventh place. They were singing Robson's name from the terraces of St James' Park. He was the new "Messiah" and he was going to lead them to the promised land.

The first step achieved, Robson could now set about making the team his own, as more of the unwanted foreign imports disappeared, and players like Carl Cort, Lomano Tresor Lua Lua, Clarence Acuña, Andy O'Brien and others came in, only for a glut of injuries to players like Shearer to deal the club a succession of cruel blows. Newcastle slipped from a high of third to a low of fourteenth before a revival saw them again take eleventh place, a huge disappointment to Robson and his team as they played to over 50,000 in their revamped ground for every home game.

But it was all bubbling under the surface, and more new arrivals, like the outstanding Jermaine Jenas and Olivier Bernard, continued to lower the average age and lift the team. After two opening draws, Newcastle galloped up the table and sat on top after beating Leeds United 4–3 at Elland Road in a typically thrilling game. That scoreline typified the season, and, although they eventually ended up in fourth place, it was enough to earn a prized place in the European Champions League the following season. Decent runs in both cup competitions ended as Chelsea managed a fifth-round victory in the Worthington Cup, while Arsenal beat them in a sixth-round replay in the FA Cup. But it was progress, and that was what Robson and his board were looking for.

London clubs had been troublesome to Robson, and an alarming number of games without a win were recorded in the capital, until he turned it around in his usual style with wins at both Arsenal and Spurs within weeks of each other.

193

> "His way of treating people both as a group and as individuals is unique."
>
> ALAN SHEARER

Suddenly, Newcastle was everyone's second favourite team (except, of course, fans of local rivals Sunderland and Middlesbrough) and their exploits in the Champions League only served to improve their and Bobby's popularity as they bounced back after three successive defeats to qualify for the second phase, only missing out on the knockout stages on the final day.

After another poor start in the Premiership, slipping down to nineteenth when they lost at Chelsea in September, and after three defeats in Europe to Dynamo Kiev, Feyenoord and Juventus, Newcastle's young team took off, beating the same three sides to qualify for the second phase of the money-spinning competition and shooting up the domestic table, never being out of the top four that season after 18 January. Home and away defeats by Barcelona ended their interest in the

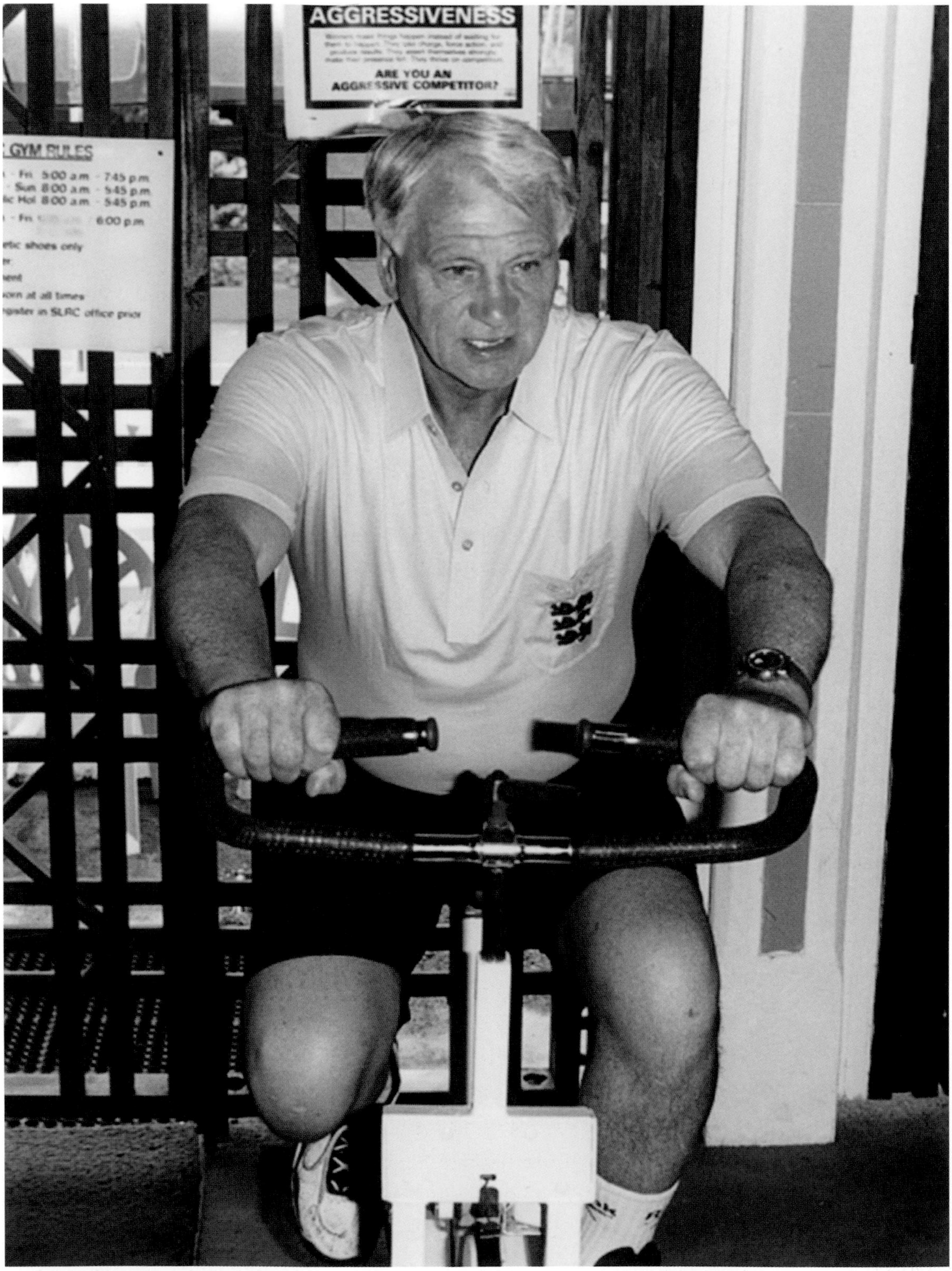
AGGRESSIVENESS
ARE YOU AN
GYM RULES

"Newcastle are very lucky to have him as a manager."

<small>PAUL GASCOIGNE</small>

Champions League, despite beating Bayer Leverkusen twice and drawing with Inter Milan.

Third place was another giant step forward as Newcastle, holding off Chelsea and Liverpool, continued to fill their ground and thrill the crowds with their adventurous attacking play.

Robson never lost his love of wingers, and the presence of Frenchman Laurent Robert and Chilean Nol Solano always ensured Newcastle would be playing attractive football as his ideal side began to take shape. The defence was strengthened by the signings of Jonathan Woodgate from Leeds United and Titus Bramble from his old club Ipswich, while the midfield was flooded with bright young things like English internationals Jermaine Jenas and Kieron Dyer, with Portugal's Under-21 captain Hugo Viana supplementing the evergreen Gary Speed. Up front, young strikers Shola Ameobi, already an England Under-21 international, and new signing Lomano Lua Lua were putting pressure on Alan Shearer and Craig Bellamy, with Michael Chopra chasing them. Chopra scored four goals in his first home game while on loan to Watford and was climbing the England international ladder at the same time.

Before the season ended, Robson added youthful midfielder Darren Ambrose from Ipswich and, given the huge gates for every home game, Premier League prize money and another tilt at the richly rewarding Champions League, there was more money available for the ever-developing Newcastle team.

Although Robson turned seventy in February 2003, thoughts of retirement were pushed even further away as he chased that elusive prize of the Premier League Championship. And Robson was not only hunting once again for silverware but, unselfishly, building a team for Newcastle's future, with every signing an investment for his successor to cash in on.

The problem was that success breeds expectation in sport and there was a demand to keep on moving onwards and upwards, not just from the vociferous Toon Army and the raucous local press but also from club chairman Freddy

195

Fighting fit. At seventy, Sir Bobby still donned a tracksuit every day and regularly worked out in the gym.

Shepherd, who seemed to have forgotten how Sir Bobby had rescued the club from relegation and financial disaster.

When Newcastle slipped out of the financially rewarding Champions League on penalties to a talented Partizan Belgrade side the reaction was to lock away the chequebook and begin a season of backbiting and complaining. The distress at losing out in such a fashion affected everyone from the dressing room to the boardroom, especially when the expected challenge for the Premiership title disappeared in the opening weeks of the season after Newcastle lost games to Manchester United, Birmingham City and Arsenal while only being able to draw with Leeds United, Everton and Bolton Wanderers. September finished with Newcastle not only out of the lucrative Champions League but also in 19th place in the League.

There was no money available for new players and an ever-lengthening injury list, but Robson, in typical fashion and in spite of his war of words with the chairman, not only battled on but somehow managed to turn it around, backed all of the time by the vast majority of the supportive Toon Army.

I recall Kieron Dyer promising Sir Bobby in the dressing room during that bleak period that Newcastle would be in the top five by Christmas. A promise made and a promise kept – for when they beat Spurs 4–0 with two goals apiece from Alan Shearer and mercurial Laurent Robert, Newcastle manoeuvred their way up the table and into the top five.

They were to hold fourth place for much of an undefeated February, but gradually the injuries took their toll, most importantly to the hugely influential Jonathan Woodgate. No new players were purchased in the January transfer window and Newcastle slipped, just enough to bring on the wrath of the chairman once again and the minority group of Magpies fans who decided they wanted Robson out – to be replaced by whom no one said!

The season finished with defeat by Marseille in the semi-final of the UEFA Cup – the furthest any English team had reached in Europe that season – while single goal defeats by Tottenham Hotspur, Bolton Wanderers and Manchester City threatened the proud Geordies and an even prouder Robson with relegation, in European qualification terms, to the Intertoto Cup.

But draws away to Southampton and Liverpool in the final two Premiership games gave Newcastle the two points they required to clinch fifth place and the chance for Sir Bobby to challenge for the UEFA Cup once again as part of an emotive last lap.

It had been a long journey over five seasons for a man who had thought his career as a football manager was over when he left PSV Eindhoven in 1998 at the end of his second spell. Sadly, it was to end sooner than he had planned. In 2004 Bobby's contract was extended for one further year – a final lap of honour before being pushed into retirement. But it was a bad start to the season and suddenly Britain's most popular manager found himself sacked after just four matches, a few days short of five years in the job.

"In situations like this there is no room for sentiment" said Chairman Shepherd. It was apparently not simply the 2–4 defeat by Aston Villa at Villa Park at the end of August extending a disappointing start to the season but also the fact he had "rested" the captain, Alan Shearer, who was playing in his final season before deciding whether to go into management or television, which had precipitated the decision.

I had spoken to Sir Bobby by telephone on the Friday from the Olympic Stadium in Athens before the game and he had told me of his intentions, saying that at 34 years of age, three games in eight days was too much for his skipper and he also needed to look at the outstanding young prospects Shola Ameobi and the recently signed Dutch superstar Patrick Kluivert. What he did not add was that Shearer had not scored an away goal from open play since November and with results as they were he needed to find some punch. He did. Newcastle scored two, but conceded four. Shearer had said he wanted to play every minute of every game

"I know we have probably the best squad of players we have assembled in many a year."

197

in his final season but, in truth, away from his own adoring fans he was not on form.

It was Robson who had extended the England striker's Newcastle career by five seasons, bringing him millions of pounds in rewards, far more than his manager earned in the same period, and extending his legend on Tyneside. But on the day of Robson's sacking Shearer was pictured in national newspapers appearing to offer little support, morally or physically, to his manager. Fair-minded Geordies who cherished both their manager and their striker were stunned to see one seemingly turn against the other. But it wasn't Shearer who sacked him. That privilege went to club chairman Freddy Shepherd, who had not wanted Robson in the first place.

198

Bobby was aware that Shepherd had criticised his appointment right from the start. He had complained he was too old to do the job – although, it was reported, not in such civilised words. Robson proved him wrong by saving the club from relegation and possible bankruptcy in his first season, taking them into the Champions League and filling the revamped St James' Park stadium to capacity for virtually every match. He was not only successful on the pitch, but off it as well. He improved the club's image and began the sale of overpaid and under-performing players signed by previous manager Ruud Gullit.

He did it in his own style, buying exciting, attacking players who, in the main, were young enough to give the next manager and the next generation a flying start. His interest was in laying the foundations for the future of his favourite club, not just for his own reputation, and he had assembled a squad packed with promise. "I know we have probably the best squad of players we have assembled in many a year," he declared with some satisfaction.

Robson, as ever, took his dismissal with immense dignity. "It has naturally stopped me finishing the job I would have wanted to have done," he said. "I have had a marvellous time… I would like to wish the club every success in the world."

A nailbiting moment. Alan Shearer remains on the bench in what turned out to be the final match of Bobby's career at Newcastle United.

"In situations like this there is no room for sentiment."

FREDDY SHEPHERD

"*If he has a go at you, which he does on numerous occasions, he is always very clever at picking you back up, putting an arm around you and telling you that you are one of his blue-chip boys.*"

ALAN SHEARER

The enthusiasm of Sir Bobby was infectious. Everyone enjoys a joke, including Alan Shearer and the fourth official (*left*), as Robson signals a substitution. Sir Alex Ferguson and Sir Bobby may have been great rivals in the game, but they were also great friends and the two knights held each other in high respect (*above*). Bobby never forgot how Alex Ferguson helped him during the tough eight years as England manager.

Sir Alex Ferguson: "I go back with Bobby to 1981 when Ipswich won the UEFA Cup. I was at Aberdeen at the time and we played Ipswich in the first round of the competition the next year and we beat them. You could see his infectious style, and, even though they lost, he came into the dressing room straight after the game – not an easy thing to do – and told us we could win the Cup and not to let him down. Unfortunately, we did, because we threw it away when we lost to Hamburg in the quarter-final.

From then on we kept in touch quite a lot, not now and again but regularly, and when he became England manager and I came down here we got on really well. It is easy to like Bobby Robson because he is a true football man. There are a lot of people in the game who are projected about what they are and what they are not but this is a pure football man, and it is easy for people like myself to relate to him, understand him and love him."

"*Players never know why they are dropped or substituted – until they become managers.*"

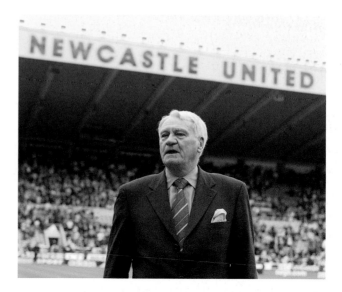

Bobby takes charge of Newcastle United for the first time, as the team take on Chelsea at Stamford Bridge (*left*), on what was an emotional day. Newcastle fans had taken every possible seat they could and when Robson stepped onto the pitch he was greeted by a huge roar from the Toon Army, followed by a standing ovation from the entire crowd.

203

"When he came to Newcastle you could see that it was his team. I mean the enthusiasm, the fighting spirit, the commitment and players having fun playing football, they enjoy it."

<small>RUUD VAN NISTELROOY</small>

204

Bobby Robson made friends wherever he went. He was just that sort of person. Passionate about football and passionate about life. You could not help but feel uplifted by the man, as his former PSV player Ruud van Nistelrooy was when the two met before Newcastle's game against Manchester United (*opposite*). You can see the pride in Bobby's face as he shows the Dutch striker the new stands at St James' Park, although van Nistelrooy looks far more interested in the man he believes kick-started his career and then helped him with his dream move to Manchester United. And how does van Nistelrooy thank him? By scoring goals against Sir Bobby's beloved Newcastle. Not a friendly gesture, but no more than Bobby expects from a player he rates as one of his greatest strikers in a long line of world-class goal-scorers he has managed over the years.

It was all looking so good. Newcastle may have beaten Partizan with a solitary Nolberto Solano goal in Belgrade but their hopes of a run in the Champions League were dealt a devastating blow in the return leg when Ivica Iliev scored from a Sasa Ilic cross to level the tie. It was then all down to penalties but in the critical shoot out, despite Lomano Tresor Lua Lua's prayers (*left*), the normally reliable Alan Shearer blasted his spot kick over the bar and Kieron Dyer's effort was saved by goalkeeper Ivica Kralj. Newcastle were eliminated.

Two former England managers battle it out (*above*), with Sir Bobby seeking a place in Europe for Newcastle, and Manchester City manager, Kevin Keegan, playing for Premiership survival. Keegan won this end-of-season encounter thanks to a single goal from Paulo Wanchope.

"All the flash cars in the car park? I don't begrudge them it, not at all. All I want them to do is appreciate it."

The birthday boys. Rising Newcastle star Jermaine Jenas and Bobby Robson (*above*) share the same birthday and the same midfield talents. Bobby had no hesitation in meeting Nottingham Forest's valuation of the teenage player, especially when the England Under-21 manager, David Platt, who was boss at the City Ground when Jenas came through, predicted not only a regular England place but also the captaincy. Bobby brought his young protégé along gradually without rushing him, and he was rewarded with sparkling displays and spectacular goals.

Bobby (*opposite*) keeps his eye on the ball as the talented Frenchman Laurent Robert bears down on the Southampton goal in their meeting at St James' Park in February 2002.

"If I had a wish, it would be to carry on managing Newcastle for another thirty years. When you look at the youth of the team what a future the club has."

Bobby loved being involved in training and took a deep interest in everything. Robson was conscious of not carrying on as manager for too long. He was unequivocal, saying that the moment he felt it slipping away he would be off – no going upstairs, no lingering on. Certainly, young players like Kieron Dyer (*opposite*), sitting on the steps during a training session, were behind him. That is why Dyer committed himself to the club when there were so many options open to him. Only a run of injuries stopped him becoming a regular member of the England team.

" *When I fell and broke a rib the doctors insisted I sat in the stand. I was too far away, out of touch and couldn't wait to get back to the touchline and my team.*"

Sir Bobby's right hand man. Alan Shearer (*above*) slots home yet another penalty, this time against Portsmouth at St James' Park, after Stefanovic had handled a Lee Bowyer shot in a three-goal victory in late October 2003.

"It's a tough world out there, and if you aren't tough, you won't survive and you won't get where you want to be."

217

Many happy returns. Sir Bobby went back to Holland to face his former club PSV Eindhoven in the quarter final of the UEFA Cup. After conceding an early goal, Newcastle battled back to equalise through Jermaine Jenas (*above*) to take a 1–1 draw back to St James' Park. In the return leg, the home side won 2–1 thanks to trademark Gary Speed header.

218

The last game. A season of frustration, injuries and sweat finally came down to this final match at Anfield where Newcastle needed a single point to clinch a valuable place in the UEFA Cup for Sir Bobby's final lap of honour. Craig Bellamy, pictured here holding off Danny Murphy, risked his health by coming back early from injury to replace the injured goalscorer Shola Ameobi. The Reds deservedly equalised through the inevitable Michael Owen but the Toon held on for the vital draw.

Rediscovering that scoring touch. Alan Shearer was convinced that his time with Newcastle United was shuddering to a halt, until Bobby arrived to resurrect his career in fantastic style. After that, the goals flowed and England yearned to have their former skipper back in the number nine shirt.

   Shearer (*opposite*) slides home a typically clinical penalty against Charlton Athletic at The Valley in March 2003.

"Life is good, we enjoy life."

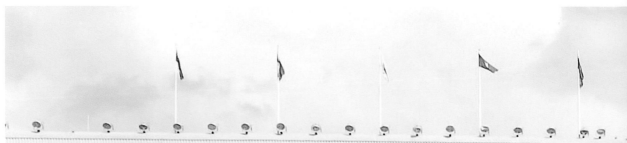

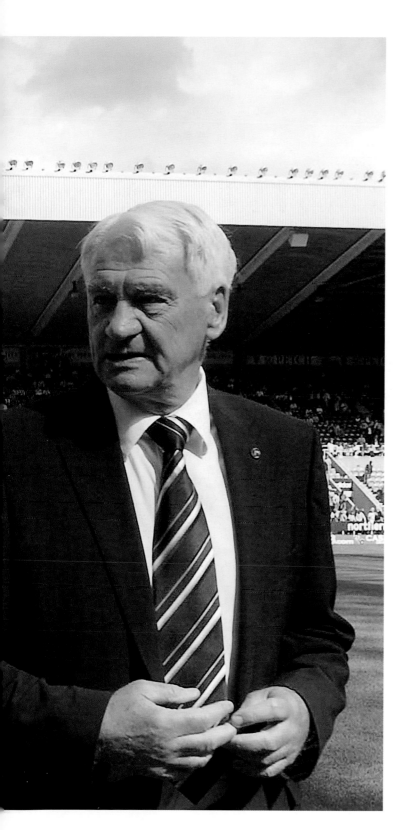

"It has naturally stopped me finishing the job I would have wanted to have done. I have had a marvellous time... I would like to wish the club every success in the world."

12 The Final Chapter

Remarkably, or perhaps not, Sir Bobby had kept his private box in the stand after his sacking, and rather than sulk and hide he not only continued to watch Newcastle but also broadened his horizons to take in another local team, Sunderland. Oil and water comes to mind, but Sir Bobby Robson was made as welcome at Sunderland as he remained at Newcastle.

Within hours of his dismissal I received a call from a club chairman desperately keen to sign him up – and that was just the start. He would undoubtedly have remained as a top line manager, certainly not as a technical director or adviser, but for the ongoing cancer problems which ruled out full-time employment.

Instead, he was happy enough to accept a job with the Irish Football Association – helping youthful manager and former Liverpool player Steve Staunton, as well as watching football and cricket, attending the many dinners and celebrations held in his honour and, typically, working for charity. He wondered why the FA hadn't found him something similar.

Ironically it was another old acquaintance of mine who replaced Robson at the helm of Newcastle United – Graeme Souness, who soon found problems in a fall-out with a couple of senior players and the vanity signing of Michael Owen from Real Madrid for a then stunning fee of £16.5 million. Just like Robson before him, Souness suffered from serious interference from the board and was gone by the end of the season.

The gentle Glenn Roeder then came and went almost unnoticed, replaced by the gritty, hardworking but unloved Sam Allardyce, who upset the fans further with his signing of enfant terrible Joey Barton from Manchester City.

Bobby watched in amazement as his club was torn to pieces, with Shepherd selling out to multi-millionaire sports shop chain owner Mike Ashley, who, to the joy of the fans, replaced the unpopular Allardyce with old favourite Kevin Keegan. But no sooner had he arrived than Dennis Wise was made executive director of football and battle commenced. It was untidy, ugly and it depressed

225

A final farewell.
Fittingly, Sir Bobby's very last public appearance was at St James' Park. He received a standing ovation.

Robson enormously. Keegan's latest return to the club ended in disaster when he left and put the matter in the hands of his lawyers.

Robson told me just weeks before his death that he felt the appointment of London-based Wise was a grave error and that the former England player had to shoulder much of the responsibility for the remarkable downturn in fortunes.

Next to arrive, again to the bemusement of Robson, was the veteran and long retired Joe Kinnear whose first act was to fall out with the local media while Chairman Ashley added to the chaos when he put the club up for sale. Kinnear then succumbed to illness and had to undergo a triple heart bypass operation, leaving coach Chris Hughton in charge of team affairs. Alan Shearer became the seventh manager in the five years since Robson was sacked. He was given just eight matches to save the club from relegation – unthinkable, when Europe had been the target for the season. He failed. On the last day of the season Newcastle were relegated and Sir Bobby looked on in amazement. "It was," he told me in another of our long telephone conversations, "No more than we deserved. It is very sad and we need a new, committed owner, a change of players and a new attitude. But I hope Shearer stays."

226

With Sir Bobby's blessing. The latest in a long line of managers, Alan Shearer watches from the sideline as Newcastle play Portsmouth in April 2009.

It was not, as some suggested, Newcastle United's 6–1 defeat by unconsidered First Division side Leyton Orient in a pre-season friendly which caused the final downward spiral of Sir Bobby Robson's life. He knew, after five debilitating, sapping bouts of invasive cancer, that the time he had left was borrowed and he said as much when I visited him a few weeks before his death at 6.30 am on Friday 31 July 2009.

That one unimportant result was just the latest of the events at St James' Park that had cut him to the quick. Relegation had been a shocking blow to a man who bled black and white stripes and he was, he told me, singularly unimpressed with some of the people holding senior positions with one of the best-supported clubs in the world, but he didn't dwell on it. Instead, he talked with great enthusiasm about the Sir Bobby Robson Foundation and how surprised he was at the way the money rolled in, from fifty pence pieces to cheques for £5,000 and more. The initial target of £500,000 to set up a dedicated cancer research centre for the disease in Newcastle was passed in a trice and he told me with great pride that his efforts had now raised more than £2 million.

But time was running out and he knew there was not a moment to waste if he was to fulfil a couple of promises to himself and other people as he made one final push towards filling the coffers of the Sir Bobby Robson Foundation to overflowing to help his treasured doctors and surgeons in their research on cancer.

Two appointments remained. The first was his charity celebrity golf tournament in Portugal and I knew what an effort this was going to be for him as he told me after an earlier visit to the same country that he could never make the trip again because it hurt so much. He not only went, much against the wishes of the good Lady Elsie, but insisted on staying on for an extra few days to make full use, he joked, of the £2,000 insurance he had been forced to pay.

The second appointment was "back home" at St James' Park, where he had arranged a game in his name between England and Germany old boys. He was near to tears when 35,000 fans turned up and gave him the longest standing ovation in the ground's history. He was wheeled around the perimeter of the pitch in his wheelchair, raising his hat, which he had taken to after chemotherapy had robbed him of much of that wonderful mane of white hair, to salute their loyalty to him.

It wasn't arranged, but Alan Shearer finished off the night in style when he scored the winning goal to make it 3–2 to England. Robson and Shearer, both as Geordie as the Blaydon Races, loved that moment. There was, quite rightly, no memory or mention of the rancour between the two just before Bobby's disgraceful dismissal.

Sir Bobby was driven back after the match to his magnificent home in the heart of Durham a happy man. His football commitments were finished, and he had helped raise five times the original target for his cancer charity, with the fund still growing. He went home to the bosom of his family and quietly passed away a few days later, according to his son Andrew, at peace and without pain. It was the final wish of all his close friends.

The outpouring of grief at his passing would have amazed the man, but he would have been delighted to know that a staggering £1.6 million, mainly in small donations, was paid into his fund between the announcement of his passing on the Friday and the following Monday morning... with a lot more to come.

Donations for the Sir Bobby Robson Foundation can be sent to PO Box 307, Heaton NE7 7QG

A moving moment.
As Bobby was
wheeled around the
pitch, he raised his
hat to the spectators
in the grandstands.

"I found it a very emotive evening... It was quite something, a fitting tribute, and something that Sir Bobby really deserved."

GARY LINEKER

230

Sir Bobby Robson and his wife, Elsie, arrive at the BBC Sports Personality of the Year Awards in December 2007. There was not a dry eye in the house as Sir Bobby went up on stage to accept his Lifetime Achievement Award, presented by Gary Lineker.

232

"There are no grey areas. He is straightforward football. You get that passion from him whenever you meet him. He is unbelievable. He is like me – the most important part of his life is football."

SIR ALEX FERGUSON

Another milestone. Sir Bobby poses with Kevin Keegan and Sir Alex Ferguson next to a bust of himself *(left)*, unveiled to mark his 75th birthday during the Barclays Premier match between Newcastle United and Manchester United at St James' Park on 23 February 2008.

Bobby's last public appearance was on 26 July 2009 at the charity match he had organised between England and Germany old boys in aid of the Sir Bobby Robson Foundation *(above)*. The match ended 3–2 to England, with Alan Shearer scoring the winning goal.

Career Record

Robert William Robson
Born: Sacriston, Co. Durham, 18 February 1933
Height & weight (1960): 5´9.5˝(177cm), 11st 10lb (74.5kg)

Clubs

Chester-le-Street Junior Football; Langley Park Juniors; Fulham, May 1950; West Bromwich Albion, March 1956 (£25,000); Fulham, August 1962 (£20,000); Vancouver Royals (player-coach) 1967-68.

Playing Career Record

Fulham	League	Cup	Goals
1950-51	1	-	-
1951-52	16	-	3
1952-53	35	1	19
1953-54	33	1	14
1954-55	42	1	23
1955-56	25	2	10
Total	152	5	69

West Bromwich Albion	League	Cup	Goals
1955-56	10	-	1
1956-57	39	9	13
1957-58	42	7	27
1958-59	29	3	5
1959-60	41	3	6
1960-61	40	1	5
1961-62	39	4	4
Total	240	27	61

Fulham	League	Cup	Goals
1962-63	34	4	2
1963-64	39	3	1
1964-65	42	5	2
1965-66	37	3	6
1966-67	41	6	-
Total	193	21	11

Complete career record

	League	Cup	Goals
	585	53	141

Playing career: England record

	Played	Won	Drawn	Lost	Goals
England	20	11	7	2	4

Playing career: England match by match

27 Nov 1957	v France	4-0	2 goals

The last midfielder to score twice on his England debut.

18 May 1958	v USSR	1-1	
8 Jun 1958	v USSR	2-2	World Cup Finals

Robson had a goal disallowed for an alleged foul on the famous Soviet goalkeeper Lev Yashin.

11 Jun 1958	v Brazil	0-0	World Cup Finals

The first goalless draw in any World Cup Finals.

15 Jun 1958	v Austria	2-2	World Cup Finals

Robson had another goal disallowed, which would have sent England into the quarter-finals.

15 May 1960	v Spain	0-3	
22 May 1960	v Hungary	0-2	
8 Oct 1960	v N Ireland	5-2	
19 Oct 1960	v Luxembourg	9-0	World Cup qualifier
26 Oct 1960	v Spain	4-2	
23 Nov 1960	v Wales	5-1	

Jimmy Greaves scored England's 1,000th goal.

15 Apr 1961	v Scotland	9-3	1 goal

Robson opened the scoring in England's biggest ever win over Scotland, and the only match in which the Scots conceded more than seven goals in a game.

10 May 1961	v Mexico	8-0	1 goal

Robson scored the third goal in Mexico's biggest ever defeat.

21 May 1961	v Portugal	1-1	World Cup qualifier
24 May 1961	v Italy	3-2	
28 Sep 1961	v Luxembourg	4-1	World Cup qualifier
14 Oct 1961	v Wales	1-1	
25 Oct 1961	v Portugal	2-0	World Cup qualifier
22 Nov 1961	v N Ireland	1-1	
9 May 1962	v Switzerland	3-1	

Managerial career record

Clubs

Fulham January – November 1968; Ipswich Town January 1969 – May 1982; England July 1982 – June 1990; PSV (Eindhoven) July 1990 – June 1992; Sporting (Lisbon) July 1992 – December 1993; Porto February 1994 – May 1996; Barcelona July 1996 – May 1997 (general manager to June 1998); PSV (Eindhoven) July 1998 – June 1999; Newcastle United September 1999 – August 2004.

Managerial Career: Season by Season

® = relegated	Lge	P	W	D	L	F	A	Pts	Pos
Fulham 1967-68	Div 1	42	10	7	25	56	98	27	22 ®
Fulham 1968-69	Div 2	42	7	11	24	40	81	25	22 ®
Ipswich 1968-69	Div 1	42	15	11	16	59	60	41	12
Ipswich 1969-70	Div 1	42	10	11	21	40	63	31	18
Ipswich 1970-71	Div 1	42	12	10	20	42	48	34	19
Ipswich 1971-72	Div 1	42	11	16	15	39	53	38	13
Ipswich 1972-73	Div 1	42	17	14	11	55	45	48	4
Ipswich 1973-74	Div 1	42	18	11	13	67	58	47	4
Ipswich 1974-75	Div 1	42	23	5	14	68	44	51	3
Ipswich 1975-76	Div 1	42	16	14	12	54	48	46	6
Ipswich 1976-77	Div 1	42	22	8	12	66	39	56	3
Ipswich 1977-78	Div 1	42	11	13	18	47	61	35	18
Ipswich 1978-79	Div 1	42	20	9	13	63	49	49	6
Ipswich 1979-80	Div 1	42	22	9	11	68	39	53	3
Ipswich 1980-81	Div 1	42	23	10	9	77	43	56	2
Ipswich 1981-82	Div 1	42	26	5	11	75	53	83	2

	Lge	P	W	D	L	F	A	Pts	Pos
PSV 1990-91	Prem	34	23	7	4	84	28	53	1

For the first time since 1934, the Dutch league title was decided on goal difference.

	Lge	P	W	D	L	F	A	Pts	Pos
PSV 1991-92	Prem	34	25	8	1	82	24	58	1
Sporting 1992-93	Prem	34	17	11	6	59	30	45	3
Sporting 1993-94	Prem	11	8	1	2	20	7	17	2
Porto 1993-94	Prem	17	12	4	1	29	5	28	2
Porto 1994-95	Prem	34	29	4	1	73	15	62	1
Porto 1995-96	Prem	34	26	6	2	84	20	84	1
Barcelona 1996-97	Prem	42	28	6	8	102	48	90	2
Barcelona 1997-98	Prem	38	23	5	10	78	56	74	1
PSV 1998-99	Prem	34	17	10	7	87	55	61	3
Newcastle 1999-00	Prem	38	14	10	14	63	54	52	11
Newcastle 2000-01	Prem	38	14	9	15	44	50	51	11
Newcastle 2001-02	Prem	38	21	8	9	74	52	71	4
Newcastle 2002-03	Prem	38	21	6	11	63	48	69	3
Newcastle 2003-04	Prem	38	13	17	8	52	40	56	5

Managerial Career: Major Trophies

Ipswich Town	FA Cup 1978, UEFA Cup 1981
PSV (Eindhoven)	Dutch League 1991, 1992
Porto	Portuguese Cup 1994, Portuguese League 1995, 1996
Barcelona	Spanish Cup 1997, European Cup-Winners' Cup 1997

Managerial Record: Winning Cup-runs

Ipswich FA Cup 1978

Cardiff City	2-0
Hartlepool United	4-1
Bristol Rovers	2-2, 3-0
Millwall	6-1
WBA	3-1
Arsenal	1-0

Ipswich UEFA Cup 1980-81

Aris Salonika	5-1, 1-3

In the first leg, John Wark became the second and last player to convert three penalties in a European club match.

Bohemians (Prague)	3-0, 0-2
Widzew Lodz	5-0, 0-1
Saint-Etienne	4-1, 3-1
Cologne	1-0, 1-0
AZ 67 (Alkmaar)	3-0, 2-4

Barcelona European Cup-winners' Cup 1996-97

AEK (Larnaca)	2-0, 0-0
Red Star (Belgrade)	3-1, 1-1
AIK (Stockholm)	3-1, 1-1
Fiorentina	1-1, 2-0
Paris Saint-Germain	1-0

No club has ever retained the Cup-Winners' Cup. Barcelona maintained that record by beating the holders in the final.

Managerial Career: England Summary

Played	Won	Drawn	Lost	For	Against
95	47	30	18	154	60

Managerial Career: European Championships

1984 European Championships qualifying matches

22 Sep 1982	v Denmark	2-2
17 Nov 1982	v Greece	3-0
15 Dec 1982	v Luxembourg	9-0
30 Mar 1983	v Greece	0-0
27 Apr 1983	v Hungary	2-0
21 Sep 1983	v Denmark	0-1
12 Oct 1983	v Hungary	3-0
16 Nov 1983	v Luxembourg	4-0

Failed to qualify for main tournament

1988 European Championships qualifying matches

15 Oct 1986	v N Ireland	3-0
12 Nov 1986	v Yugoslavia	2-0
1 Apr 1987	v N Ireland	2-0
29 Apr 1987	v Turkey	0-0
14 Oct 1987	v Turkey	8-0
11 Nov 1987	v Yugoslavia	4-1

1988 European Championships

12 Jun 1988	v Rep. Ireland	0-1
15 Jun 1988	v Holland	1-3
18 Jun 1988	v USSR	1-3

Eliminated after round one

Managerial Career: World Cup

1986 Qualifying matches

17 Oct 1984	v Finland	5-0
14 Nov 1984	v Turkey	8-0
27 Feb 1985	v N Ireland	1-0
1 May 1985	v Romania	0-0
22 May 1985	v Finland	1-1
11 Sep 1985	v Romania	1-1
16 Oct 1985	v Turkey	5-0
14 Nov 1985	v N Ireland	0-0

Finals

3 Jun 1986	v Portugal	0-1
6 Jun 1986	v Morocco	0-0
11 Jun 1986	v Poland	3-0
18 Jun 1986	v Paraguay	3-0
22 Jun 1986	v Argentina	1-2

Eliminated in quarter-finals

1990 Qualifying matches

19 Oct 1988	v Sweden	0-0
8 Mar 1989	v Albania	2-0
26 Apr 1989	v Albania	5-0
3 Jun 1989	v Poland	3-0
6 Sep 1989	v Sweden	0-0
11 Oct 1989	v Poland	0-0

Finals

11 Jun 1990	v Rep. Ireland	1-1
16 Jun 1990	v Holland	0-0
21 Jun 1990	v Egypt	1-0
26 Jun 1990	v Belgium	1-0 aet
1 Jul 1990	v Cameroon	3-2 aet
4 Jul 1990	v West Germany	1-1 aet (lost 4-3 pens)

4th place

Index

A

Acuña, Clarence 192
Allen, Ronnie 32, 33
Ambrose, Darren 195
Ameobi, Shola 195, 197, 218–19
Arnesen, Frank 153, 176
Arsenal 53, 165–6

B

Barcelona 65, 101, 154, 166, 170–71, 172–89, 193, 213, 214–15
Barnes, John 103, 128
Baxter, Bill 64
Beattie, Kevin 64, 67, 69, 76–7, 90–1
Beckenbauer, Franz 101, 134
Bellamy, Craig 195, 218–19
Benfica 163, 164, 165, 166
Bernard, Oliver 193
Bramble, Titus 195
Brazil, Alan 64, 66
Buckingham, Vic 31–2, 33, 34–5, 44
Butcher, Terry 64, 66, 81, 88–9, 112–13, 128, 142–3
Byrne, Roger 41, 42

C

cancer 23, 166, 168, 225, 227, 228
Carroll, Tommy 64
Carruthers, John 64
Champions League 154, 193, 195, 196, 198, 207
Charlton, Bobby 41, 43
Cherbakov, Sergei 163, 164

Chopra, Michael 195
Clarke, Allan 35, 56, 60
Clough, Brian 65, 107
Cobbold, John 57, 63, 68
Cobbold, Patrick 63, 68
Cohen, George 35, 58, 59
Cooper, Paul 64, 67, 78–9
Cort, Carl 192
Costinha, Paulo 164
Cruyff, Johan 173, 174
Cruyff, Jordi 174

D

Da Costa, Pinto 164, 165–6, 168
Derby County 65
Dodgin, Bill 12–13, 19
Dorjee, Hans 153, 156, 158
Dyer, Kieron 195, 196, 207, 212–13

E

Edwards, Duncan 41, 42
England national team 22, 32, 33, 41–51, 100–49
Everton 65, 164, 176

F

FA Cup 63, 66, 75, 92
Ferguson, Alex 154, 158, 201, 232–33
Ferguson, Bobby 81, 88–9, 92, 94–5
Figo, Luis 163, 173, 175, 182
Finlay, George 64
Finney, Tom 41, 42, 46–7, 49
Fulham 12–13, 18–29, 34–5, 55–6, 59

G

Gascoigne, Paul 64, 90, 91, 103, 140–1, 145, 146–7, 195
Geddes, David 64, 65
Gerets, Eric 153, 154, 176
Gilliland, David 10, 15
Greenwood, Ron 22, 32, 102, 106–7

H

Hagan, Jimmy 31
Hateley, Mark 103
Haynes, Johnny 20, 21, 24–7, 34, 35, 40, 41, 43, 45, 56
Hill, Jimmy 21, 22, 26, 33–4, 103, 131
hooliganism 33, 101–2
Howe, Don 32–3, 34–5, 41, 44, 50, 105, 108–9, 132, 137, 138–9
Hunter, Allan 63, 64, 67

I

Ipswich Town 56, 57, 62–99, 143, 176
Irish Football Association 225

J

Jenas, Jermaine 193, 195, 208, 217
Jezzard, Bedford 20, 24–7, 34
Johnson, David 64, 67, 69

K

Keegan, Kevin 101, 207, 225–6, 232–3
Kluivert, Patrick 197

L

Langley Park Juniors 10–11, 13, 17
Lee, Robert 192
Leeds United 65
Lineker, Gary 6–7, 103, 104, 105, 110, 127, 128, 137, 145, 146–7, 230
Lofthouse, Nat 42
Lua Lua, Lomano 192, 195, 206–7

M

Manchester United 33, 65, 154, 158, 174, 200
Maradona, Diego 101, 104, 127
Mariner, Paul 80, 81
Marsh, Rodney 35
Matthews, Stanley 42
Middlesbrough 12
Miller, Eric 55, 56
Millichip, Bert 33, 118, 151
Mills, Mick 64, 67, 76–7, 98–9, 102
Moore, Bobby 43, 48, 49, 50, 51
Mourinho, Jose 163, 165
Muhren, Arnold 65, 66, 84–5, 151
Mullery, Alan 34, 35, 56

N

Newcastle United 9, 10–11, 12, 18, 22, 91, 176, 190–223, 225–7

O

O'Brien, Andy 192
Osborne, Roger 64, 66, 67, 75
Osman, Russell 64, 66
Oxford University 44

P

Pearce, Stuart 105, 145
Platt, David 104, 144, 145, 208
Ploegsma, Kees 152, 156
Porto 163, 164–71

press criticism 101, 102, 109, 151, 173–4, 179
PSV Eindhoven 105, 151–61, 176

R

Ramsey, Alf 41, 44, 57, 70, 101
Raul 180
Revie, Don 60, 65
Robert, Laurent 195, 196, 208–9
Robson, Andrew 228
Robson, Bryan 103, 104, 121
Robson, Elsie 22–3, 31, 33, 53, 227, 230
Robson, Keith 10
Robson, Lillian 8, 9, 12
Robson, Phil 10
Robson, Philip 8, 9, 10, 11, 12, 18
Robson, Ron 10, 13, 16
Robson, Thomas 11, 16, 64
Romario 151–2, 153
Ronaldo 156, 157, 174, 175, 182, 186
Rous Cup 137

S

Sexton, Dave 56–7, 65, 105, 114–15
Shearer, Alan 192, 195, 196, 198, 200, 201, 207, 216, 220–21, 226, 228, 233
Shepherd, Freddy 191, 195–9, 225
Shilton, Peter 104, 110, 128
Solano, Nol 195, 207
Southampton 12
Southend 53
Speed, Gary 195, 217
Sporting Lisbon 163–4, 165, 166
Sunderland 12, 65, 225

T

Talbot, Brian 64, 65, 66, 67, 76–7

Taylor, Graham 101, 106, 107
Taylor, Tommy 41, 42
Thijssen, Frans 65, 66, 84–5, 86, 151
Tyrell, Ray 64

U

UEFA Cup 63, 66–7, 81, 85, 86, 164, 168, 196–7, 217, 218

V

Valckx, Stan 153, 154, 163
van Aerle, Barry 153
van Bruekelen, Hans 153
van Gaal, Louis 173, 175, 180, 188–9
van Nistelrooy, Ruud 154, 158, 159, 204–5
Vancouver Royals 35, 53–5
Venables, Terry 106, 107, 178, 179
Viana, Hugo 195

W

Waddle, Chris 105, 128, 145, 146–7
Wark, John 64, 85
West Bromwich Albion 23, 30–9, 42
Wilkinson, Howard 96, 97, 108–9
Wilson, Tom 13, 19, 21, 23, 32
Winterbottom, Walter 22, 41, 44
Wise, Dennis 225, 226
Woodcock, Tony 110
Woodgate, Jonathan 195, 196
World Cup (1958, Sweden) 42–3, 49
World Cup (1962, Chile) 43–4, 49, 50, 51
World Cup (1966, England) 41, 44
World Cup (1986, Mexico) 101, 103–4, 118, 121, 123, 126–7
World Cup (1990, Italy) 7, 101, 104–5, 134, 141, 144–5, 151

237

"In life, you know you cannot succeed and be clever and be bright and be correct and be spot-on all of the time, because life is more complicated than that, life is more difficult than that."

238

Fans' tributes at Ipswich Town's Portman Road stadium included this scarf hung around the neck of the Sir Bobby Robson statue.

Acknowledgements

Bob Harris would like to offer sincere thanks to Lady Elsie Robson and Sir Bobby's family for their patience and kindness to an old hack over many years; Sir Bobby's tireless PA Judith Horey; Jane Morgan; Paul Clark; Mike Dunn; Mike Shapow in the USA; Jonny Dexter; Matt Lowing; Debbie Woska and publisher Michael Dover.

Picture Credits

Action Images: 2, 30, 35, 45, 52, 67, 69, 77, 84, 105, 135, 136, 142, 161, 186, 190, 200, 201, 205, 206, 208, 209, 212, 214–15 (all), 218, 219, 221, 222.

Bob Harris: 1, 7, 8, 10, 13, 14, 16, 17, 194, 240.

Getty Images: 199, 226 (Newcastle United), 229 (Newcastle United), 230, 231, 232 (Newcastle United), 233 (Newcastle United), 238.

Popperfoto: 4, 18, 24, 25, 26, 27, 28-29, 36-37, 38, 39, 40, 46-47, 48-49, 50, 51, 54, 58, 59, 60, 61, 62, 68, 68 (both), 70, 71, 72-73 (all), 74, 74-75, 76-77, 78-79, 80, 81, 82, 85, 86, 87, 88, 90, 91, 93, 94-95,96, 97, 98-99,100, 106 (both), 107, 108, 110, 112-12 (all), 114, 116-117, 118, 119, 120, 121, 122, 123,124-125, 126,127, 128, 130, 131, 132, 134, 138, 140, 141, 144, 145, 146, 148, 149, 150, 155 (Reuters), 156 (Reuters), 157, 158 (Reuters), 159, 162, 167, 168, 169, 170, 172, 177 (Reuters), 178, 179 (Reuters), 181, 182 (Reuters), 183, 184, 187, 189, 202, 210, 213, 216, 217.

Steve Drew/Press Association Images: 224.

First published in the United Kingdom in 2003
by Weidenfeld & Nicolson.

This edition first published in the UK in 2009
by Weidenfeld & Nicolson

10 9 8 7 6 5 4 3 2 1

A CIP catalogue record for this book is available from the British Library.

ISBN 978 0 297 85927 7

Design Director: David Rowley
Project Editor: Matthew Lowing
Editor: Claire Wedderburn-Maxwell
Designer: Nigel Soper

Printed and bound in Italy.

Weidenfeld & Nicolson
The Orion Publishing Group
Orion House
5 Upper Saint Martin's Lane
London WC2H 9EA

An Hachette UK Company

The Orion Publishing Group's policy is to use papers that are
natural, renewable and recyclable products and made from wood
grown in sustainable forests. The logging and manufacturing
processes are expected to conform to the environmental regulations
of the country of origin.